WHEN YOUR CHILD TURNS FROM

D1494348

GOD

Help and encouragement for parents of prodigals

Dorothy Eaton Watts

REVIEW AND HERALD®
PUBLISHING ASSOCIATION
HAGERSTOWN, MD 21740

The author assumes full responsibility for the accuracy of
all facts and quotations as cited in this book.

Texts credited to Clear Word are from *The Clear Word,* copyright © 1994,
by Jack Blanco.
Texts credited to NIV are from the *Holy Bible, New International Version.*
Copyright © 1973, 1978, 1984, International Bible Society. Used by
permission of Zondervan Bible Publishers.

This book was
Edited by Jeannette R. Johnson
Interior design by Patricia S. Wegh
Cover design by Matthew Pierce
Typeset: Caslon 224 Book 12/13.5

PRINTED IN U.S.A.

00 99 98 97 96   5 4 3 2 1

R&H Cataloging Service
Watts, Dorothy Eaton, 1937-
    When your child turns from God: help and encouragement for
parents of prodigals.

    1. Apostasy.   2. Evangelistic work.   3. Conversion.   4. Spiritual life.

                253.5

ISBN 0-8280-1065-X

DEDICATION

Dedicated to
Stephen, Esther,
and David,
who have
given me
the incredible
privilege,
adventure, and joy
of being their mother.

CONTENTS

Chapter One

YOU ARE NOT ALONE

After trying to have children for seven years, Marj and Tom finally chose to adopt. While they were going through the necessary paperwork, close friends advised, "You should leave well enough alone. Children will cause you more pain than they're worth. Give up the idea if you want to save yourselves a lot of trouble later on."

Marj and Tom shook their heads in disbelief. How could children bring anything but love and joy to the hearts of parents? Didn't God plan that we should have children? Surely all you needed to do was to love your children, raise them correctly, and you would live happily ever after.

They looked at parents with wayward children and told themselves, "That will never happen to us! We will be perfect parents. We'll do it right. There's nothing to worry about!"

A number of years later, when their children became teenagers, someone gave them a motto that they hung on their bedroom wall: "Insanity is inherited. You get it from your children!" By then Marj and Tom knew what it meant to see a child rebel, making choices that broke their hearts.

"What did I do wrong?" Marj asked herself. "If only I had been more strict, or more loving, or more watchful, or more understanding, or more informed. Surely there is something I could have done to prevent this!"

"If only I hadn't been on the road so much," Tom lamented.

"If only I'd spent more time with the kids."

Marj and Tom began to argue, each blaming the other for what had gone wrong. Then, needing each other so much, they made up and wept before God together. "Lord, forgive us for not being the parents we should have been. Please bring our children back to You before it is too late."

Feeling guilty for not raising perfect children, Marj felt near despair. She resigned her church offices and withdrew from social functions. Her sense of failure in parenting made her feel like an outcast of society.

Parents of prodigals

Marj and Tom are not alone. They are but two of thousands of parents since time began who have had the same hope, prayed the same prayer, and felt the same anguish. This book will share the stories of more than 65 prodigals and their parents. Some prodigals are well-known historical figures: Aurelius Augustine, John Newton, Adoniram Judson, and Hudson Taylor. Some are well-known Christian leaders of this century: James C. Dobson, Sr., Franklin Graham, Dick Eastman, and Glenn Aufderhar. Others are known to few besides their parents. Each prodigal had parents who hurt because of their actions. Each had parents who prayed for them unceasingly.

After reading about these parents of prodigals, you will know that your pain is not unique. You hold no monopoly on parental anguish, heartbreak, and disappointment. Others have experienced the frustration, discouragement, and hurt you are going through. God did not forsake them or their children. He will not forsake you and yours.

We will tell stories of prodigals who returned and tales of others who are still in the far country. We will share with you how other parents coped with their hurt, what practical steps they took to restore relationships, and how they learned to pray with power. These stories will not only give you hope, but will suggest concrete actions you can take, actions that can make a difference in your life and the lives of your adult children.

All of the stories in this book are true. When first and last names are used, sources for the information are listed. When only first names are used, the story is still true, but the name and certain identifying details have been changed to protect the people involved.

This book is for you

Have you felt as if your heart were breaking as you watched a child become involved in a non-Christian lifestyle of drugs, promiscuity, drinking, or smoking? Have you felt discouraged as you have watched a child stop attending church? Have you known the intense pain of learning that your child is in a homosexual relationship? Have you wept as your child, raised to love God, now laughs at your faith and mocks God's Holy Word?

Have you felt a stab of fear when the telephone rings in the middle of the night? Do you look forward to family gatherings with a mixture of joy and apprehension? Do you sometimes feel like a battle-scarred warrior in your search for peace with one of your adult children?

Have you lain awake until dawn trying to sort out where you went wrong as parents? Have you found it hard to hold back the tears when you see other parents speak in glowing terms about their children who are workers for God? You are not alone. This book is for you.

This book is for parents who hurt because of choices their adult children have made. It is for parents who pray for prodigals who have wandered from God and the church.

A common problem among Christian parents

"How often I have agonized about my failure as a mother!" Pam Caruso writes. "Though I did what I thought was best in rearing my children to know and love God, as they reached maturity one by one they chose to live their lives apart from Him. This despair I feel is not mine alone. Many other Christian mothers, some of whom are the most godly women I know, express the same turmoil of spirit."[1]

If it is true that many Christians are parents of prodigals, then why do we so often try to keep our own pain hidden? Why do we look at others smiling in church and decide that we have a monopoly on pain?

Perhaps we're afraid to share our burdens because we feel somehow that we are to blame. We feel we are failures as parents and don't want others to know that we are grappling with the shame of a child who has gone astray. But we are not alone!

I well remember how I felt when one of our children rebelled against values we had tried so hard to teach. It hurt so bad! I cried until I had no more tears to shed. I felt a complete failure as a parent and as a Christian. Everyone else seemed to have succeeded as a parent, while I alone had failed.

Many years later I see things differently. I know now that most of my fellow church members have also been parents in pain. Oh, the crisis points have been different, but the hurt has been similar. We have ached with the frustration of what we feared was our inadequacy as parents. We tried so hard! What did we do wrong?

I can now praise God for His presence during those long-ago times of crisis. I can look with pleasure at the transforming work of God in our family. The children who gave us pain now give us much joy! We thank God for each of them and for His power working in their lives.

I pray that the stories in this book will help remove any sense of isolation you may feel as parents of prodigals. You'll discover that your experience is a common one among dedicated, loyal, loving Christian parents.

These stories will affirm what you've known all along but somehow forgotten: that God never leaves your side. He understands what you are going through, for He too is a parent in pain. He walks with you in your sorrow. He will yet cause your heart to sing with joy!

Along the same lines, Pam Caruso writes, "Even as I cry out to God in my deepest pain, I remember that He understands. He has been there! He was perfect, yet one third of His angels chose to live apart from Him. Even Adam and Eve had a son who chose not to follow God, though he had been to the gate of the Garden of Eden and knew the story of his parents' fall. I do not suggest that I have been a perfect mother. Yet my heavenly Father knows that I did my best, and He understands and weeps with me. It gives me courage and hope to know that the One who gave His only begotten Son to redeem me knows my pain." [2]

No longer alone

Ralph and Margie Lewis became anxious when Mark didn't

come home for supper. By calling around to his friends they discovered he had left for Florida that morning on his Honda. They searched his room for clues. There was nothing. *Why had he left without telling them? Why had he gone off halfway through his college term? Was he in some kind of trouble? Where was he? What was he doing?*

That night Ralph and Margie lay awake listening to the silence of the night, hoping to hear the roar of an approaching motorcycle that would signal the return of their son. The sound never came. Every day they went through the motions of living for the sake of their other two children, but the worry about their 19-year-old prodigal choked them with fear. He never wrote. He never called.

A family friend phoned and reported seeing him in West Palm Beach, where he was working in a motel. She said that he was OK, but that he had asked her not to contact them.

Months went by without a word. The family went to visit the grandparents in Florida, as they had planned. They took along gifts for Mark, expecting he would show up there for Christmas dinner. He didn't show. He didn't call.

At last, in desperation, they got out the yellow pages and began calling motels. They went from motel to motel, showing his picture, asking if anyone had seen him. No success. When they were just about to give up hope they spotted his Honda. Ralph went in to inquire while the others sat in the car. He came back a few minutes later, alone. He had talked briefly with Mark, but Mark wouldn't come to the car. He wanted them to leave.

Margie later wrote about that experience. "Outside, I cried. Inside, I hurt like I had never hurt before."[3]

Mark eventually came home and relationships were restored, but as a result of their painful experience they found themselves more open to other hurting parents, less willing to criticize, more ready to encourage and support. They began to experience what John White calls "the fellowship of parents in pain."[4] With Mark's permission, Margie wrote her testimony in *The Hurting Parent.*

Some time after the book was published, the mother of a son with a drinking problem wandered through a flea market.

She stopped at a table of used books, where Margie Lewis's book caught her eye. The crowds surged around her as she began to read. She hadn't gone far before she knew she had to have that book.

Taking it home with her, the mother read it through twice, then lent it to a friend, who was also a hurting parent. When it wasn't returned, the woman bought another copy from a Christian bookstore and read it a third time.

She wrote her appreciation to Margie. "My problems are far from over. But at least now I know I'm not going crazy. And I'm not alone."[5]

That story expresses the purpose of this book—to encourage parents of children who have wandered from God and the church. To encourage *you*. To give you hope. To help you know that you are are not alone.

What can I do now?

1. In their book *What Did I Do Wrong? What Can I Do Now?* William and Candace Backus outline three types of problems with adult children: chronic, crisis, and criminal.[6]

   a. Chronic Problems:
      emotional problems
      rebellion
      severe interpersonal conflicts
      homosexuality
      addictions
      inability to keep a job
      dishonesty
   b. Crisis Problems:
      pregnancy
      attempted suicide
      expulsion from school
      dismissal from employment
      runaway from home
      divorce
      separation
      illness
      accident

c. *Criminal Problems:*
   drug dealing
   drug possession
   theft
   assault
   rape
   murder
   prostitution
   fraud
   abuse

Try to think of someone you know who has one or more of the problems listed under each category above. Write their name, and the name of their child (if you know it), beside each problem.

Take time to pray for each parent in pain that you have listed. Ask God to give encouragement and hope to each one today.

2. *Try to find two or three other hurting parents to join with you to form a prayer group for prodigals.* "Prayer and Love Saves" is a seminar available through AdventSource, 5040 Prescott Avenue, Lincoln, NE 68506. 800-328-0525.

The "Prayer and Love Saves" seminar has everything you need to lead a prayer support group to encourage parents of prodigals: sharing exercises, a 15-minute presentation on the topic, parent showcase stories, handout masters, small group Bible study questions, group discussion questions, and ideas for prayer time. The seminar covers the same topics as the ones in this book, but sometimes from a different perspective. Although written by the same author, only about a third of the material is the same. The book, *When Your Child Turns From God,* and the seminar, "Prayer and Love Saves," have been written to complement each other.

Hope from Bible parents

1. Read the stories of the following parents in the Bible who hurt because of the behavior of their children. List the problem behaviors. How would you classify the problems the parents faced?

   a. Adam and Eve (Gen. 4)
   b. Isaac and Rebekah (Gen. 25:20-34; 27; 28:1-9)

c. Jacob and Leah (Gen. 34)

d. Eli (1 Sam. 2; 3; 4)

2. Read the passages below. It will be more effective if you choose only one text per day for your meditation. Read the chapter in as many versions as possible. Underline the texts that speak especially to your heart.

What does each passage tell you about God as a hurting parent, and His ability to understand your pain? What does each reveal about how God deals with His wandering children?

a. Isaiah 43

b. Hosea 11

c. Isaiah 49

d. Jeremiah 31

e. Psalm 103

---

[1] Pam Caruso, "He Understands," in Rose Otis, ed., *The Listening Heart* (Hagerstown, Md.: Review and Herald Pub. Assn., 1993), p. 230.

[2] *Ibid.*

[3] Marjorie M. Lewis with Gregg Lewis, *The Hurting Parent* (Grand Rapids: Zondervan Pub. House, 1988), pp. 19-28.

[4] John White, *Parents in Pain* (Downers Grove, Ill.: InterVarsity Press, 1979), p. 244.

[5] Lewis, p. 14.

[6] William and Candace Backus, *What Did I Do Wrong? What Can I Do Now?* (Minneapolis: Bethany House, 1990), pp. 18-24.

Chapter Two

THE
BLAME
GAME

Susanna Wesley set about to be the best possible mother she could be to her 19 children. As soon as they were born, she began to train each of them by strict, methodical principles. From their birth she trained their wills, teaching them to cry softly and to always obey. They were never allowed to eat between meals, and they followed a regular plan for eating, worship, and sleeping. She operated a home school for six hours every day, as well as spending one hour per week with each child, instructing him or her in biblical principles. In addition, she still managed to set them an example by spending two hours every day in her own personal devotions.[1]

"Susanna Wesley's home at Epworth was an almost perfect Christian household," observes Edith Deen. "Few mothers in history have possessed the spiritual sensitivity, the stamina, and the wisdom of Susanna Wesley."[2]

Out of such an exemplary home came two well-known Christians: John Wesley, founder of Methodism, and Charles Wesley, hymn writer. Another son, Samuel, was also a minister. However, few know about her other children who brought her pain. Four of her daughters had disappointing marriages—Patty, Kezzy, Sukey, and Emilia. Another daughter, Hetty, fell in love with a smooth-talking womanizer. She ran away from home to be with him. He got her pregnant, but refused to marry her. Hetty came home in disgrace and was quickly married to a local plumber.

Susanna felt not only betrayed by Hetty, but forsaken by God. She had done her best to bring them all up in the way they should go. *How could a loving God let this happen to one of my children when I have tried so hard to do everything right? What more could I have done?* Susanna wondered.[3]

Myth 1: Children who are taught right will never rebel.

Susanna Wesley believed the myth that children who are taught right will never rebel. She based her belief on a misunderstanding of Proverbs 22:6. But this verse doesn't say that a child will never go through the "prodigal son" stage, rebelling against God and family. It does promise that the child will never be able to forget the lessons learned in childhood.

One missionary mother, a very spiritual woman who gave much thought and prayer to training her children in the way they should go, wrote in her diary, "We can expect God to honor us by not allowing our children to rebel." Yet one of her children chose to wander from God and the church.

Can you imagine the agony of soul as that mother cried out to God, "Why, God, why? We did our best! How could You let this happen after what You have promised in Proverbs 22:6?"[4]

But this is not a promise that a child will never go wrong. Rather, "it is a statement, a *general* statement, about how family relationships normally work," says John White.[5]

The book of Proverbs is a collection of wise sayings. As you read through them you will discover there are many statements about children who rebel against the counsel of their parents. As John White explains, "parents are admonished to bring up children properly. Children are admonished to respond wisely to parental correction. If both play their part, all will be well."[6]

The facts are that there are wonderful Christian households in which children were trained correctly, but they chose to rebel. In the parable of the lost son, does Jesus condemn the father whose son went to the far country?

If this myth were true, it would make God a bad parent, because one third of the angels chose to rebel against His love, goodness, and right training. God has made all His creatures with the freedom of choice.

Myth 2: Parents are responsible for the sins of their children.

This myth was circulating in the days of Ezekiel. There was a proverb going around that said, "The fathers eat sour grapes, and the children's teeth are set on edge."

After questioning Ezekiel about this proverb, the Lord set the record straight. He said, "As surely as I live, declares the Sovereign Lord, you will no longer quote this proverb in Israel. For every living soul belongs to me, the father as well as the son—both alike belong to me. The soul who sins is the one who will die" (Eze. 18:1-4, NIV). In verse 20 God continues, "The son will not share the guilt of the father, nor will the father share the guilt of the son" (NIV).

"So then every one of us shall give account of himself to God" (Rom. 14:12). No child in the judgment will ever be allowed to blame his or her parents for choices made with his or her own free will. God has it straight about who is responsible for the choices each has made.

Of course, as parents, we will be held accountable. But for what are we accountable? What is our responsibility? We are responsible for training, being an example, loving unconditionally, and praying for our children. We are not responsible for the child's attitudes, feelings, choices, and sins.

Was Cain's murder of Abel blamed on his parents? Was Samuel blamed for the sins of his sons? Did God blame Jacob for the behavior of Dinah? Was the prodigal son's father charged with the sins of his son in the far country?

Billy Graham understood where his responsibility as a parent ended. At 22 his son Franklin was smoking, drinking, and following other worldly pursuits, but Pastor Graham refused to take the responsibility for his son's choices.

In 1974 the Grahams were in Lausanne, Switzerland, for an International Conference for Evangelism. On Franklin's birthday Billy and Ruth took him to lunch. After lunch Billy walked with his son along the lake. After some time of nervous silence he turned to Franklin and said, "Your mother and I sense there's a struggle going on in your life."

Franklin made no response.

His father continued, "You're going to have to make a

choice either to accept Christ or reject Him. You can't continue to play the middle ground. Either you're going to choose to follow and obey Him, or reject Him."

Still Franklin said nothing.

"I want you to know we're proud of you, Franklin," Billy continued. "We love you, no matter what you do in life, and no matter where you go. The door to our home is always open, and you're always welcome. But you're going to have to make a choice."

Silence was Franklin's only response. But inside he knew that he alone was responsible for his sins, and he alone could decide what to do about them.

A few weeks later he sat on his bed in a hotel room in Rome, lit a cigarette, picked up a Bible, and read John 3. The words of his father came back to him. "Franklin, you are going to have to make a choice to accept Christ, or reject Him." Franklin crushed out his cigarette, knelt, and gave his life to God. That night the Grahams' prodigal returned home.[7]

Myth 3: Parents must rescue their wayward children.

Parents who believe this myth pay the fine when a child is arrested for driving while under the influence. They pay the bills when a child's rent comes due, or he or she can't make payments on a new car. They cover up for a child's mistakes and hope that their benevolence will help the child do better. Says Lee Ezell, "Somehow we've got to stop paying the price for our 'of-age' kids. . . . We must come to the place of allowing them to reap the consequences and eat the bitter fruit of their own wrong choices."[8]

Remember the story of the lost son? Did the father go after his son, pay all his bills, refusing to allow him to suffer the consequences of his choices? No, he allowed the consequences to bring the boy to his senses.

Tough love refuses to replace what children have destroyed, to cover up and lie for them, to make excuses for their behavior, to bail them out when they get into trouble, and to pay their debts for them. Tough love refuses to accept the blame for choices children have made.

Billy and Ruth Graham had tough love for their rebellious son Franklin. When he got into trouble with the law, his parents let him face the consequences. One day Franklin raced past Pete Post, who was parked beside the highway in his police car. Franklin figured Pete would recognize his green Triumph Spitfire, know that he was Billy Graham's son, and look the other way. He was wrong.

Pete pursued, his cruiser lights flashing. Franklin stepped on the gas and sped up the mountain to his home, pushed the remote control button to open the gate, then closed it behind him. He laughed as he imagined the look on Pete's face when he found the gate closed. Telling no one about the incident, he went to his room.

His joy didn't last long. In a few moments Billy called Franklin to come downstairs. He said, "Pete Post is on his way up. I've opened the gate for him. You and I are going to have a meeting with him. If he wants to arrest you, I'm going to support him."

Ruth nodded her agreement.

Pete gave Franklin a stern lecture about safe driving and promised to take his license and put him in jail if he ever caught him speeding again.

About that experience Franklin writes, "I learned something that I had not known before: If I got into trouble and was wrong, I couldn't count on my daddy to fix it or defend me. I never forgot his promise to stand with Pete Post, even if it meant seeing me dragged off in handcuffs."[9]

"Whatsoever a man soweth, that shall he also reap" (Gal. 6:7). God allows the law of cause and effect to play itself out; so should we.

Myth 4: Our children belong to us; they are ours.

False. Our children are gifts to us from God (Ps. 127:3). They are given to us in trust; they are on loan. They are not ours; they belong to Him. He loves them more than we could ever love them. We can trust them into His care.

Barbara Johnson tells about a woman who struggled through two years of terrible depression after learning that her daughter Carol was in a lesbian relationship. At last she could stand it no longer. In desperation she took her burden to God. She prayed, "Carol is *Yours* more than she is mine, and I know that You love her more than I do. So, God, *You* take care of her. You know how to reach her where I cannot. I can't carry this burden any longer, so I'm giving it to You."

She not only laid down her burden, but left it there. God gave her peace and the ability to sleep at night.[10] Carol's mother understood the beautiful truth that God loves our children so much that He will never stop seeking them. There is nowhere they can go that is beyond His reach.

"It does not matter that these wanderers refuse to listen, or that they will not attend church, or that they become silent when the conversation turns to spiritual things. It does not even matter if they refuse to read the Bible or pray. What matters is that they cannot escape from God, who is everywhere and who is always speaking."[11]

Our children have wandered not only from us and our values, but from the fold of God. Our child is His child, His lost sheep. He is the Good Shepherd who is out there in the night and the storm, searching for His precious lost one. We can trust Him to search until He finds.

Gloria Gaither agrees. She writes, "It always calms the storm of parental worry to know that God loves our children infinitely more than we can, because He is the perfect parent with perfect love. I am able to be with and to help my children only to the limit of my presence. But there is no boundary to His presence."[12]

Myth 5: It is possible to be a perfect parent.

False. The truth is that no human parent is perfect. "All have sinned, and come short of the glory of God" (Rom. 3:23). There are no righteous parents, no not one (verse 10). We have all sinned against our children. None of us have done everything right. Often we have sinned unwittingly. We did things the way our parents did things. Maybe only now, after many years, do we understand what we should have done, or not done. Hindsight seems to be better than foresight.

After raising three children, Madeleine L'Engle writes, "Sometimes Hugh and I feel that if we have done anything right with our children it has been an accident and a miracle; often we realize, in retrospect, that the things we thought were best weren't really very good at all. Perhaps our children have taught themselves more on our mistakes than on our good will." [13]

The glory of the gospel is that "if we confess our sins, he is faithful and just to forgive us our sins, and to cleanse us from all unrighteousness" (1 John 1:9).

God is on our side in this business of parenting. "And if any man sin, we have an advocate with the Father, Jesus Christ the righteous: And he is the propitiation for our sins" (1 John 2:1, 2). Jesus died for imperfect parents, as well as for wandering children. His blood can cover our sins as well as theirs. He will be a perfect parent to our children, making up to them where we may have failed them.

Myth 6: Parents can control the destiny of their children.

Jan Johnson had recently given birth to her first child, Jenna. "Mother, how can I be sure Jenna will be saved and go to heaven with me?" she asked.

Her mother, Evelyn Christenson, replied, "Nothing you can do, Jan, will guarantee that Jenna will go to heaven. That is strictly a personal decision every person must make—no matter who their parents are or what ritual or rite of passage they have gone through." [14] Evelyn Christenson understood that we can never control another human being, even when that person is our own child.

This is a difficult concept for many parents to grasp. John White wrestled with this when he and his wife were considering having a second child. He came to the point of praying, "Lord, if this child will not grow up to serve You, then I would rather do without."

"What about Adam and Me?" God whispered to John's heart. "I did not make him a robot, but created him in My image. I gave him the ability to please Me or displease Me, to obey Me or to disobey. I knew the choice he would make, yet I brought him to life."

John felt God was saying to him that day, "John, are you willing to give the gift of life to your child, no matter how your child might choose to use that life? You cannot have control over what the fruit of your body will do with the life you give. Are you willing to do as I did, to give life to someone who might bring you humiliation, pain, and disgrace?"

It was not easy for John, but he prayed, "Yes. Give me the power to beget another child . . . whatever course that child may eventually choose in life." [15]

What can I do now?

1. Rewrite each myth so that it is a statement of truth about parenting. For example, the opposite truth for myth 6 might be stated: "The ultimate destiny of our children rests in their own power of choice."

2. Find a quiet spot where you will not be distracted. Take a blank sheet of paper and write down all the mistakes you have made as a parent. Be as specific as you can be. When you have finished your list take it to God in prayer, confessing each wrong, asking Him to forgive.

Read the following texts as God's answer to your prayer of confession: 1 John 1:9; Isaiah 1:18; Psalm 103:8-11.

Take a match and set fire to the paper. As you watch it burn, ask God to burn away the guilt of past mistakes from your mind and give you the assurance of His love.

3. Read Joel 2:18-32 in several different versions. Underline at least eight promises for imperfect parents. Praise Him now for the great things He is going to do in your family.

4. Read Joel 2:1-17 in the same versions as above. Underline at least eight things God asks imperfect parents to do in order that He might work on behalf of them and their families. Have you done what God wants you to do?

Hope from Bible parents

Read the story of Samuel's sons in 1 Samuel 8:1-7. Read about his grandchildren and great-grandchildren in 1 Chronicles 25:5 and 2 Chronicles 5:11-13. Also, read the commentary on this story in *Patriarchs and Prophets,* pages 604 and 605. Then decide on an answer to each of the following true or false questions. What support in Scripture do you have for your answer?

1. Samuel felt hurt because his children did not follow his godly example.

	True	False
	O	O

2. The people blamed Samuel
for the unruly conduct of
his sons.

    True   False
    O   O

3. Samuel had failed to
teach his sons the correct
value system.

    True   False
    O   O

4 Samuel felt hurt because
of the effect of his son's
behavior on his leadership.

    True   False
    O   O

5. Samuel had been a
perfect parent.

    True   False
    O   O

6. God's promise to Samuel
was not fulfilled in his
sons, but in his grandchildren.

    True   False
    O   O

---

[1] Edith Deen, *Great Women of the Christian Faith* (New York: Harper and Brothers, 1959), pp. 141-149.

[2] *Ibid.,* p. 141.

[3] Sandy Dengler, *Susanna Wesley* (Chicago: Moody Press, 1987), pp. 181-187.

[4] John White, *Parents in Pain,* p. 42.

[5] *Ibid.,* p. 43.

[6] *Ibid.,* p. 44.

[7] Franklin Graham, *Rebel With a Cause* (Nashville: Thomas Nelson, Inc., 1995), pp. 118-123.

[8] Lee Ezell, *Pills for Parents in Pain* (Dallas: Word, 1992), p. 117.

[9] Graham, pp. 56-58.

[10] Barbara Johnson, *So, Stick a Geranium in Your Hat and Be Happy!* (Dallas: Word, 1990), p. 86.

[11] Tom Bisset, *Why Christian Kids Leave the Faith* (Nashville: Thomas Nelson, Inc., 1992), p. 209.

[12] Ezell, p. 137.

[13] Madeleine L'Engle, *A Circle of Quiet* (San Francisco: Harper Collins, 1992), p. 116.

[14] Evelyn Christenson, *What Happens When We Pray for Our Families* (Wheaton, Ill.: Victor Books, 1992), pp. 47, 48.

[15] White, pp. 56-58.

Chapter Three

LETTING GO

Lass, a 2-year-old border collie, crouched in the dirt. Ears laid back, she snarled and snapped as Phillip Keller approached. He took note of the two chains that restrained her. One led from her collar to a steel post; another led from her neck to her back leg, making movement almost impossible.

"I can't do a thing with her!" the owner complained. "She jumps fences, chases cars, and terrorizes the neighborhood. I've got to get rid of her."

She was pretty old to begin training, but Phillip Keller looked into the sad eyes of the dog and knew he had to try. *You're an intelligent dog. I feel sorry for the way you've been treated,* Phillip thought. *You could make a wonderful sheepdog. I think I'll try to help you.*

Lass didn't show gratitude. All the way home she lay behind the seat of the car and growled, baring her teeth when Phillip tried to touch her. At his ranch he provided a fine kennel, good food, sparkling water, and a long chain so she could exercise. However, Lass refused to enter the kennel. She refused to eat or drink or to allow Phillip to pet her. She began to lose weight.

Understanding the dog's longing, Phillip set her free. She bolted for the woods. For several days she remained hidden. Then one evening she appeared on top of a large rock behind the house. When Phillip called her name, she ran from him. He took food and water to the rock; the next morning it was gone. For several weeks he left food and water for her. Each night it disappeared.

I wish she'd come to me, Phillip thought. *I wish she'd get to know me, to trust me, to learn to love me, to work with me, to be my friend.*

One evening Phillip stood alone outside his house in the golden sunset, watching his sheep graze. It was a beautiful scene, and he stood there entranced, his hands clasped behind his back. Suddenly he felt a soft warm nose touch his hands. Lass had come home. In the fading twilight she followed Phillip home, quietly entered her kennel, and lay down to rest.[1]

How like Lass we all are! God offers to take us into His family. He provides for our every need. He lovingly calls our name. But He sets us completely free. No chains hold us to Him against our will. We must return to Him because of our own free choice.

How like Lass our children are! And we parents who love them so much must somehow learn to do with them what God does for us, what Phillip Keller did for Lass. We must set them totally free. Letting go of our children is perhaps the most difficult task parents have to face with their adult children.

Carol found it extremely difficult. She raised six children, two from a first marriage, and four from a second. After nearly 30 years of mothering, she admitted she had a problem turning off her skills and "letting go of being a mother hen."

She looks back over the years and realizes she had a tendency to hang on to her control. She says, "I did the footwork for my kids when they should have done it for themselves. I remember when one of my sons was looking into colleges. He needed help finding the right resources, but I didn't just help him—I did the entire thing for him. I'm like that."

When her children expressed a need, she responded quickly with an idea, a book, a thought, a piece of advice. She replaced things for her children that were broken or worn out, blocking the reality of the consequences.

Then Carol's grown daughter became pregnant and moved back home. It was a difficult situation, and Carol struggled to let go, allowing her daughter to make her mistakes, to grow and mature. But the holding-on habit of a lifetime was hard to break.

She prayed daily, "She's in Your hands, Lord. Help me to keep my hands off. Help me to let go and let You do Your job!"[2]

Most of us, like Carol, find it very hard to let go of our children physically, emotionally, and spiritually.

> As children bring their broken toys
>   with tears for us to mend,
> I brought my wandering child to God,
>   because He was my friend.
> But then, instead of leaving Him
>   in peace to work alone,
> I hung around and tried to help
>   with ways that were my own.
> At last, I snatched him back and cried,
>   "How can You be so slow?"
> "My child," He said, "what could I do?
>   You never did let go."
>   —*Adapted, with apologies*
>   *to the unknown author.*

There are at least eight ways we seek to hang on to our adult children: pleasing, rescuing, being a martyr, manipulating, correcting, anger, clinging to false hopes, and continuing the parenting role. Let's look at each of them.

Let go of pleasing

Eighty-three-year-old Ethel controls her grown children by trying to always put them first, pleasing them, giving up for them. She doesn't express her own needs, but gives herself to the needs of her children. She has made it her life to be sweet, pleasant, and unreal.

One of her children says, "She controls us by being sweet, putting us first, deferring her own needs. But sometimes it makes me mad. I feel as if I'm always walking on eggs around her."[3]

Pleasing can interfere with our relationships. We need to release ourselves from the need to control through pleasing. We don't need to anticipate and meet every need of our children. We don't need to spend more time, money, and emotional energy on our adult children than we spend on ourselves. Our children's approval should not be the goal of our existence.

Let go of rescuing

Bill is always there for his adult children, sending them checks to help with dental bills and house payments. If anything goes wrong, his kids know where they can go. Bill is a rescuer.

Emily is always available as a baby-sitter for her grandchildren. If the kids need anything the parents can't provide, Grandma is there to get it for them. They'll never lack for clothes, toys, or spending money as long as Grandma is there. She is the family rescuer.

We parents need to let go of the idea that it is our duty to take care of whatever children can't handle. We need to stop rescuing them from pain in order to win their affection. We need to stop feeling guilty if our children need help that we can't afford to give. We don't have to supply all the needs of our children. We can let go and let God do that. Our children need to learn to trust Him just as do we.

Karen O'Connor was a rescuer. She was the "good old mom" who was always there when her children needed her. She was the type to put on a party for her teenagers, to run to the library to return their overdue books, to take their turn at doing dishes when they had other plans, and to help them with last-minute assignments. She began to wake up when her children were grown and the pattern was still going on.[4]

Karen joined a prayer support group for parents after she began having difficulties with her grown son. Everything she tried to do to help him was met with rejection. After listening to Karen's story, a woman on the other side of the room got up and went over to Karen, putting an arm around her shoulder. "Your work in the flesh is over," the woman said softly. "All he needs now are your prayers."

"Do you mean I don't have to do anything?" Karen gasped. "I don't need to wire him money or send food or get him another car or look into a treatment program for him? All I need to do is pray?"

The concept of letting go in order to let God work was a new idea for Karen, but she determined to try it. She found that not only was it a great relief, but better still, it worked!

Let go of being a martyr

Martyrs are always suffering. They let everyone know about their fear, fatigue, hunger, aches and pains, and mental anguish. They need only get sick or feel bad, and children will rush to their side to make them happy, to give attention.

Martyrs make children feel guilty for not doing more for them "after all I did for you children." Martyrs use their physical or mental condition to garner sympathy and exercise a form of control over their children, keeping them by their side.

We need to let go of our martyrdom. We need to grow up ourselves, depending on God instead of our children. We need to stop trying to exercise control by making children feel that they owe us something, even if it is simply their gratitude.

Let go of manipulation

Manipulation is another form of control that some of us are not beyond using. Arlene insists that her grown children come home for Christmas every year. She tells them, "It just isn't Christmas unless you are all here." If one of them has other plans, she puts on pressure. "But the others are all coming. You don't want to spoil everyone's Christmas!"[5]

Eighty-five-year-old Henry is a manipulator. If his daughter doesn't phone every week, he gets into a stew. He calls her and says, "You'll miss me when I'm gone!" He isn't even beyond using mention of his fasting and prayers on her behalf to try to get her to see things his way.

We need to let go of manipulation of our adult children. We need to let go of using guilt and shame to get what we want. We need to let go of the feeling that our children owe us.

Let go of the need to correct

It's easy for us to see the mistakes of our children, to want to give advice, to correct those mistakes, even when the children are grown up. After all, if we don't tell them what's wrong with them, how will they ever change? When we point out faults, we say "It's for your own good."

Criticism makes a child feel stupid. In actuality the parent is saying to his adult child, "You aren't as smart as I am. You can't see that you are doing it wrong. Listen to me, and you'll do better." Adult children resent parents who find fault and point out error. Much as Lass pulled against the chains of her old master, so our adult children pull away from us when we try to control through correction.

Criticism is destructive of a relationship with our adult children. We need to let go and let God do any correcting that needs doing. He will do it when the time is right, and with just the right amount of love and caring.

Let go of anger

Betty was angry. The more she thought about the reckless behavior of her son, the madder she got. She was upset that he had given up going to college, had just quit a good job, and was ruining his life with alcohol and drugs. Life just wasn't fair. Other parents hadn't tried half as hard as she to be a good mother, and then this was the reward she got.

She felt justified in her anger. Her son's behavior warranted her reaction. However, the relationship kept getting worse until she let go of her right to be angry and came to the place of forgiveness of her son.

Let go of false hopes

Cameron had waited long for a son. He put his whole life into that boy. He had such high hopes for him: He would grow up to be a great man, a physician who would take over Cameron's practice when he was ready to retire.

But his son hated medicine. He tried the premed course and dropped out. He loved mechanical things, cars, old machines. He got a job in a repair shop. But every time he came home for a visit, his father kept talking about his going back to college, finishing medicine, taking over his practice.

It's time for us to give up our dreams for our children and let them have their own dreams. It's time for us to forget our fantasies about the magic moment when our children will become what we had always dreamed they would be.

Let go of our parenting role

Frederick Buechner discovered how difficult letting go is when one of his daughters became anorexic. He and his wife begged, cajoled, and implored her to eat, but she stubbornly refused. She starved herself until her face looked like a skull and her body was little more than bones covered with skin. To Frederick, she looked like a victim of Buchenwald.

Frederick loved his daughter so much that his whole life became caught up in her problem. If she ate a slice of toast, he exulted; if she ate nothing, he was in the pits. As a parent, he felt he should be able to fix things, to make them right for her. But he discovered he could no longer do that.

He writes, "I didn't have either the wisdom or the power to make her well. None of us has the power to change other human beings like that, and it would be a terrible power if we did."

Eventually he came to realize that "the only way she would ever be well again was if and when she freely chose to be. The best I could do as her father was to stand back and give her that freedom, even at the risk of her using it to choose for death instead of life."[6]

But even when he realized that he had to let go, it was almost impossible to do. When his daughter was finally hospitalized, he and his wife were thousands of miles away and were unable to try to protect her, to make her decisions, or to manipulate the events for her good. She had to face her difficulty on her own with doctors, nurses, psychiatrists, and judges who could show her tough love. She came through the experience with healing and wisdom.[7]

When he later visited his daughter in the hospital, Buechner says he felt "the passionate restraint and hush of God" and began to understand how God, our heavenly parent, deals with each of us, His stubborn children, who seem to be bent on self-destruction. He writes, "The power that created the universe and spun the dragonfly's wing and is beyond all other powers holds back, in love, from overpowering us."[8]

We need to do the same for our precious wandering children.

It's not easy!

No one ever promised parenting would be easy. Perhaps the hardest part is relinquishing our adult children to God, letting go of our control, putting them into His control. The "Moriah experience" is what Karen Burton Mains calls it.[9] Like

Abraham, we painfully climb the hill of parenthood and release the future of our child into the hands of a loving God. It was hard for Abraham; it is hard for us.

"Prayers for our children are often painful because we discover that we don't want to let go," writes Karen O'Connor about her experience of trying to relinquish her adult son. "We may believe it is safer to cling to a familiar past than to trust in a new future."

After Karen's "Moriah experience," she experienced a transformation in her relationships and now encourages parents to "offer Him your anger and fear, hate, bitterness, and disappointment. He will replace them with peace, trust, love, serenity, and contentment. And He will take on the responsibility of bringing the perfect result."[10]

What can I do now?

1. Gather photos of your children. Put the photos in a small box with a lid. Write a letter to God, deliberately returning each child to Him. Put the letter in the box with the photos. Wrap the box as a gift. Offer it in prayer to the One who loves your children more than you could ever love them. Put the box where it can remind you often that they belong to Him, not to you.

2. Write out an ACTS prayer, in which each letter of the word "acts" stands for one part of your prayer: adoration, confession, thanksgiving, and supplication.

Adoration. Praise God for the wonderful heavenly parent He is to you, His wandering child. Praise Him for His compassion, mercy, grace, and love. Praise Him for His patience and the freedom He grants you to follow or reject Him.

Confession. Confess your lack of wisdom and faith. Confess your anger, guilt, bitterness, disappointment, and frustration. Confess your critical spirit and your desire to control.

Thanksgiving. Give thanks to God for the gift of your child. Thank Him for continuing to work in your child's life.

Supplication. Offer your children back to God. Ask Him to intervene in the lives of your children, to break the power of evil in their lives, and to help them experience God's incredible love.

Hope from Bible parents

1. Read the story of Abraham's Moriah experience aloud (Gen. 22:1-18), making the substitutions that follow. (I find it a tremendously moving experience and trust it will be the same for you.)

a. Wherever it says Abraham, read your own name. If you are a mother, replace mother for father in the story, and she for he.

b. Wherever it says Isaac, read the name of your child. If the child is a girl, replace daughter for son, girl for lad, and she for he.

c. Replace "a ram caught in a thicket by his horns" with "Jesus Christ nailed to the cross of Calvary."

---

[1] Phillip Keller, *Lessons From a Sheep Dog* (Dallas: Word, 1983), pp. 13-55.

[2] Karen O'Connor, *Restoring Relationships With Your Adult Child* (Nashville: Thomas Nelson, Inc., 1993), pp. 69, 70.

[3] *Ibid.*, p. 51.

[4] *Ibid.*, p. 56.

[5] *Ibid.*, p. 91.

[6] Frederick Buechner, *Telling Secrets* (San Francisco: Harper Collins, 1991), pp. 23-27.

[7] *Ibid.*, p. 28.

[8] *Ibid.*, pp. 28, 29.

[9] Karen Burton Mains, *With My Whole Heart* (Portland, Oreg.: Multnomah Press, 1987), p. 82.

[10] O'Connor, p. 178.

Chapter Four

FACING YOUR FEELINGS

Parents of prodigals often feel like a ship's captain struggling to keep a vessel afloat on a stormy sea. Dark clouds of fear and despair block out the sun. Anger and bitterness thunder in their souls. Waves of shame and regret wash over them. Winds of rejection pierce their hearts. And sometimes the emotional elements come with the fury of a cyclone.

Like an oil tanker broken apart on hidden rocks, some parents are torn open by the rebellion of the ones they love. They are crushed by insensitivity and ingratitude. They are pounded by remorse and grief. And all too often their broken spirits spill out hurtful words.

That pretty well describes what happened to Barbara Johnson when she discovered her son was gay. Her whole world turned upside down. Conflicting emotions battered her heart. In an emotional outburst, frenzied words tumbled out. "I would rather have you be *dead* than be a homosexual!" At the same time she loved him so much. She flung herself across her bed and cried for hours. She gasped for air, choking on her sobs.

For 11 months Barbara grieved the loss of the son she had loved for 20 years. He had turned into a stranger, and she wished she could die so the pain would go away. For months she hid in her bedroom most of the day, unable to go on with life.

If God loves me, why would He let such an awful thing happen to me? she thought. *I might as well kill myself.* She got in her car and headed for a nearby viaduct. She'd decided to drive over the edge and that would be the end of her pain.

By the time she reached the top of the viaduct, however, she decided to pray instead. In her mind's eye she imagined a cross, her son, and a hammer. She told the Lord, "I'm going to nail that kid to the cross because I can't handle this anymore. . . . I thought I gave it all to You long ago. But this time I'm saying that I'm really nailing him to the cross; I'm giving him to You, and if he never comes home and I never see him again, *whatever, Lord, whatever happens,* I'm nailing that kid to the cross and giving him to *You!*"

Suddenly it seemed to Barbara that a "million little sparkles" were released inside of her. The pain and heaviness were gone. The emotional storm clouds lifted; the waves of her spirit grew calm. For the first time in 11 months Barbara felt peace.[1]

On that memorable morning Barbara Johnson's negative feelings were transformed into positive emotions as she began to apply biblical principles for handling the storms of life.

Principle 1: Contact with God transforms our emotions.

Has not God promised in Isaiah 61:3 to give us "beauty for ashes, the oil of joy for mourning, [and] the garment of praise for the spirit of heaviness"?

Jesus has a balm for every emotional sore spot. He can give us joy for our depression and peace for our pain. We may not be able to control feelings of anxiety, anger, or shame; but He can! He can exchange love for hate and hope for despair.

That morning on the viaduct Barbara made contact with God. She writes, "I not only relinquished Larry to God, I handed over all my guilt as well and knew real forgiveness."[2]

The transformation was immediate. She took a deep breath and began to sing "The King Is Coming!" One after another she sang praise songs all the way home. The next day she cleaned house for the first time in 11 months. She put on some praise records and sang with them as she went about her tasks.[3] Contact with God transformed Barbara Johnson's negative emotions into positive ones.

Principle 2: God understands our feelings.

Jesus sympathizes with parents. He notices our tears. He is touched by our anguish. He identifies with our pain. He too has wept over a lost child. This principle is based on Hebrews 4:15: "For we have not an high priest which cannot be touched with the feeling of our infirmities; but was in all points tempted like as we are, yet without sin." He suffered emotional pain, injustice, rejection, loneliness, and grief. He longed for human acceptance. He too cried for His prodigals.

One morning I was particularly burdened for our three grown children. Each of them was going through difficult times, and there seemed so little I could do. I had prayed for them so much, and still they were having problems. I wanted to fix things for them, as I had been able to do when they were small.

I cried out to God in my frustration, "Lord, where are You? Don't You see? Don't You care about my children? Have You forgotten about them?"

God answered in the words of Isaiah 49:15 and 16: "Can a woman forget her sucking child, that she should not have compassion on the son of her womb? yea, they may forget, yet will I not forget thee. Behold, I have graven thee upon the palms of my hands."

Tears came to my eyes, and a warm feeling of the presence of Christ came over me. It was as though He was whispering to my troubled heart, "Yes, Dorothy, I care about your children. I have not forgotten them. See? I have tattooed their names on My hand, along with yours!"

I placed my hand on the blank page of my prayer journal and traced around it with my pen. Then I wrote the names of my children across the hand: Stephen Andrew Watts, Selvie Esther Rupert, David Raja Watts. Under it I wrote, "God's tattoo of love!" The warmth of that moment stayed with me through the week. Many times since, as I have brought the names of my children to Him in prayer, I have imagined seeing the names of my precious ones on God's hand. I know He loves them so much that He will never forget them nor let them go. God understands your feelings, too!

Principle 3: God can supply the emotional needs of parents.

Struggles with problem children can deplete our feelings of

self-worth, power, and control. Children aren't always the comfort in old age that we had hoped. Often our anxiety level is increased by their problems. We feel weary of the battle, drained of energy.

God wants to meet our needs as parents, emotional as well as physical. He never intended that our children should supply all our needs; He has promised to do that for us. He can provide us with strength to face any problem and give relief from the tensions of parenting.

A difficult year of my life was the year I taught school in Kitchener, Ontario, while my husband returned to his work in Bangalore, India. We had planned this separation to help our three teenage children adapt to North American culture. Although we both felt it was God's will, it was harder than I expected.

About halfway through the year a serious problem came up, and I didn't think I could handle it alone. I needed my husband, so even though he had told me not to spend money on phone calls, I put one through to India.

"You've got to come home!" I wailed. "I can't handle this on my own. I need you!"

"Dorothy, I can't come. We'll have to depend on the Lord to work everything out," Ron replied. "I'll be praying for you."

I slammed down the receiver. I was angry. I didn't want to depend on God. I wanted my husband! I ran to my bedroom and cried half the night. But I had nowhere else to turn, so I turned to God for my emotional support. He did not let me down.

I walked for hours that year, sometimes spending half the day walking in the woods, talking over my problems with the Lord. He filled the emptiness. He saw me through. He helped me cope.

I often sang my prayers as I walked. I had a little tune that I used, making up different words to express whatever was on my mind that day. It went something like this:

> Dear Lord, I'm feeling so lonely,
> Dear Lord, I'm feeling so lonely,
> Dear Lord, I'm feeling so lonely,
> Thank You for helping me cope.

> Dear Lord, I give You my Stephen,
> Dear Lord, I give You my David,
> Dear Lord, I give You my Esther,
> Help them, oh, help them, dear Lord.

I found that singing and praising God for my children was a wonderful tonic for negative emotions. And guess what? I survived. So did our marriage. So did our children. When I was able to hand over my negative emotions to the Lord, He was able to take control and supply all my emotional needs for 10 months.

John and Lorrie White also turned to the Lord to supply their emotional needs when one of their five children went astray. They knew what it meant to have police cars pull into their driveway, to wait with dread to hear what the men in blue would report. They spent many nights sitting together in silence with a mutual pain too deep to express in words.

John writes, "We have found God in a way and to a degree we never did before. We have found that He too is a parent who is willing to share the secrets of all parenting, who, in fact, invented the very institution. . . . In Him we found healing and peace. By Him we learned day by day how to cope with impossible problems."[4]

Principle 4: God can use people to help us.

After his experience on the road to Damascus, Paul needed guidance. The Lord could have sent an angel, but instead He chose to use Ananias to counsel and pray with Paul. In the same way, God can bring people into our lives with whom we can share and pray about our problems. This may be a pastor, a physician, or a Christian counselor. When we have a broken leg, we do not hesitate to seek the best medical advice available. So if we have damaged emotions, or feel we are unable to cope with feelings from our past, we should not hesitate to seek professional help. In answer to our prayers for help, God will lead us to someone who can guide us.

Sometimes that help may be in the form of friends with similar problems who get together to share their burdens and to pray for one another. "Confess your faults one to another, and pray one for another, that ye may be healed," advises James (James 5:16).

Clarice is one who has experienced the encouragement that comes from fellowship with other hurting parents. After four years of meeting weekly for sharing, Bible study, and prayer with two other women, she testified how the fellowship had helped her live through the shame and despair over her rebellious children.

She told them, "I don't think it's humanly possible to cope alone with a son who's on court probation and methadone treatment for heroin addiction. Without your support and concern, without your willingness and ability to feel with me, I would have had a nervous breakdown. Our fellowship has been my only survival."[5]

Ask God today to lead you to one or two select individuals who can help share your burdens for your wandering children.

Principle 5: Feelings follow actions.

"And when they began to sing and to praise, the Lord set ambushments against the children of Ammon, Moab, and mount Seir, which were come against Judah; and they were smitten" (2 Chron. 20:22).

The Israelites must not have felt victorious when faced with the superior forces of the enemy, but they went to battle singing the song of victory. The feeling of victory followed their conscious choice to step out in faith and act out victory.

Praise and thanksgiving are ways many parents have dealt with their discouragement about their wandering adult children. It's amazing what miracles God begins to work when we stop complaining about our kids and begin to thank Him for the children He has given us, to praise Him for them, in spite of how they live and what they say. So praise God for your children, whether you feel like it or not, and God will supply the feeling.

Ruth Bell Graham is one who knows that thanksgiving and praise can do wonders, even when you don't feel like it. One night Ruth lay awake thinking about her prodigal son Ned. She thought about the struggles she had had with his older brother, Franklin, who had been rebellious. He had started out smoking, but ended up causing trouble at school and getting hauled in by the police. Now her fifth child, Ned, was also turning away from the values of their home. He was involved in drugs, and she was terribly worried.

Realizing there would be no more sleep that night, she turned on the light and reached for her Bible. The verse she turned to was Philippians 4:6: "In everything by prayer and supplication with thanksgiving let your requests be made known unto God. And the peace of God, which passeth all understanding, shall govern your hearts and minds through Christ Jesus."

She says, "Suddenly I realized the missing ingredient to my prayers had been thanksgiving. So I sat there and thanked God for all that Ned was and all he had meant to me through the years. As I began to thank the Lord, I realized worry and work were mutually exclusive. When we're most concerned, we should start thanking the Lord for the lessons He is teaching us through the tough times. And invariably, it's during those tough times that the Scriptures really come to life."[6]

When Ruth went through the motions of thanksgiving and praise, the feelings of gratitude and joy followed. This principle of "acting as if" has many applications for hurting parents. In God's strength we can perform acts of love toward our prodigals, when inside we feel like wringing their necks! God will supply the emotions of love if we step out in faith and do the deeds of love. That is the gospel, pure and simple. God will do for us what we cannot do for ourselves.

We may hurt so badly that we feel as though we could never forgive what they have done. However, in God's power we can go through the motions of forgiveness, asking God to give us the feeling of forgiveness. He will not fail us!

Principle 6: We can choose how we will feel.

"Choose you this day," said Joshua. When God made us, He created us with the power of choice. He gave us the last say in the matter of what we will do with our lives. We can choose life, or we can choose death. We can choose to be negative, or we can choose to be positive. We can choose to be happy, or we can choose to be miserable.

"Pain is inevitable, but misery is optional" is the title of the first chapter of Barbara Johnson's *So, Stick a Geranium in*

Your Hat and Be Happy. She says, "We can choose to gather to our hearts the thorns of disappointment, failure, loneliness, and dismay due to our present situation, or we can gather the flowers of God's grace, unbounding love, abiding presence, and unmatched joy."[7]

The Johnsons lost one son in Vietnam, another was killed by a drunk driver, and a third son announced that he was a homosexual. About the same time she discovered she had diabetes. In spite of all her troubles, she made a choice to change the only thing she could—her own attitude.[8]

Barbara had learned what Dr. Viktor Frankl observed while in a concentration camp during World War II. He and his sister were the only members of his family who survived. He wrote, "Everything can be taken from a man but one thing—the last of the human freedoms: to choose one's attitude in any given set of circumstances, to choose one's own way."[9]

What can I do now?

1. Read through this list of negative emotions: anger, anxiety, bitterness, depression, despair, discouragement, envy, fear, frustration, grief, guilt, hatred, jealousy, low self-worth, pessimism, rage, regret, remorse, self-pity, shame.

Underline the ones you have felt recently in connection with one of your adult children. Why do you feel that way? Write out the reasons in one or two paragraphs.

2. Write a list of the negative emotions you have felt recently. Opposite each one write the positive emotion that you would like to have to replace it. Example: hatred—love, frustration—peace, guilt—forgiveness.

3. Offer each negative emotion to God in a palms-down, palms-up prayer. Follow these steps:

    a. Place your palms down, as though you are throwing something away. Give each negative emotion to God with your palms down. Act out 1 Peter 5:7.

    b. Place your palms up, as though you are ready to receive a gift from God. Ask Him to supply the positive emotions you need.

4. Using a concordance, search for Bible verses that promise the very positive emotions you desire. Read each verse in several versions. Using 3 x 5 cards, write out at least one promise for each positive emotion. Put these in strategic places where you can read them often.

Hope from Bible parents

Read the story of Abraham, Sarah, Hagar, and Ishmael in Genesis 21:8-20. Read it several times, in different versions if possible, until the story is very clear in your mind.

1. Divide a sheet of paper into four columns. At the head of each column write the name of one of the four main characters of this story. Put yourself in the place of each character. Try to feel what they must have felt. Write down all the emotions each person felt, positive and negative.

2. Find an illustration in this chapter for each of the six biblical principles for dealing with negative emotions:

    a. Contact with God transforms negative emotions.

    b. God understands our feelings.

    c. God can supply our emotional needs.

    d. God can use people to help us.

    e. Feelings follow actions.

    f. We can choose how we will feel.

---

[1] Barbara Johnson, *So, Stick a Geranium in Your Hat,* pp. 35-48.

[2] *Ibid.,* p. 94.

[3] *Ibid.,* pp. 47-49.

[4] John White, *Parents in Pain,* pp. 14-16.

[5] Marjorie M. Lewis with Gregg Lewis, *The Hurting Parent,* pp. 44, 45.

[6] Dale Hanson Bourke, "Tough and Tender Moments," *Today's Christian Woman,* Nov./Dec. 1991, p. 50.

[7] Johnson, p. xi.

[8] *Ibid.,* pp. 1-5.

[9] Carolyn Huffman, *Meditation on a Rose Garden* (Nashville: Dimensions for Living, 1995), p. 18.

Chapter Five

UNDER-STANDING TEMPERAMENTS

Blanche Pease, a well-organized woman, often told her daughter LaVonne, "It takes more energy to throw your coat on the bed and hang it up later than to put it in the closet in the first place."

"She was absolutely right, if she meant physical energy," LaVonne agrees. "She was right about mental energy, too, if she was talking about herself. But my personality is different from hers, and for me to direct my attention to hanging up coats, when I was totally involved in some other project, required an outlay of mental energy that my mother could not imagine."

Can you understand the frustration Blanche faced during the 19 years she tried to teach LaVonne to be orderly? LaVonne married, but that did not change her personality. Can you imagine the frustration Blanche felt when she visited her married daughter's home?

"It was 10 years before I finally developed a system that provided a reasonably clean house," LaVonne admits. "Finally Mother was able to come for a visit without even once throwing up her hands and exclaiming, 'How can you live like this?'"[1]

Twenty-five years after I had married and established my own home I can remember my mother saying to me, "How can you make such a mess when you cook? My mother taught me to have a pan of hot water ready to wash up the dishes as I went. That way, when the meal was done I'd have a clean kitchen."

"I know," I'd chuckle, "and although you've told me that for as long as I can remember, I just can't do it. You might as well give up. I'm never going to learn."

It wasn't that I'm a slow learner; I'm just put together differently than my mother. She looked at my way of doing things and shook her head, muttering, "That's not the way I taught her!"

And I now find myself looking at the way my daughter keeps house and muttering to myself, "She didn't learn this from me!" Sometimes it makes me feel as though I completely failed in my role as mother until I remind myself that we have two very different personalities.

I am highly choleric—I want things done right now, this minute! I gathered my children around the table at the same times each day for meals. They had their baths on schedule, worship on schedule, and were in bed by 7:00 p.m. so that they could arise at 6:00 sharp the next morning.

Esther has a phlegmatic temperament. Her household is run in a relaxed manner. You can't set your watch by her mealtimes or bathtimes. But who's to say my way was better? Her children are happy, healthy, and much loved. She is a good mother.

People are all different. Just as no two snowflakes have the same design, so no two individuals have the same combination of genes, chromosomes, and DNA. Each of us is a unique human being, with our own fingerprint, footprint, and voiceprint. We don't all think alike, communicate alike, or socialize in the same way. We see things differently, hear things differently, and feel things differently. Understanding these differences can help us have better relationships.

In this chapter we will focus on the differences in temperaments and how these differences affect relationships with our adult children.

Four temperament types

When Jesus was on earth, He studied the temperaments of those with whom He worked. I have been amazed at how much Ellen White, a nineteenth-century Christian author, has to say about the importance of understanding these basic differences in people. She often speaks about the differences in character traits or dispositions. (We can easily substitute the more modern terms of *personality* or *temperament*.) Here are a few examples.

"The Saviour knew the character [personality] of the men whom He had chosen; all their weaknesses and errors were open before Him; . . . and His heart yearned over these chosen ones."[2]

"When he [Judas] came into association with Jesus, he had some precious traits of character [personality traits] that might have been made a blessing to the church."[3]

"The apostles differed widely in habits and disposition [temperament]. . . . The fiery zealot Simon; . . . the generous, impulsive Peter, and the mean-spirited Judas; Thomas, truehearted, yet timid and fearful, Philip, slow of heart, and inclined to doubt, and the ambitious, outspoken sons of Zebedee. . . ."[4]

We can see in these disciples examples of what we today call the four basic temperament types: sanguine, choleric, melancholy, and phlegmatic.[5]

1. Sanguine. Generous, impulsive Peter is an example of the sanguine personality. Sanguines are spontaneous, in the middle of everything, quick to speak their mind, unafraid of taking the limelight, easily hurt, but quick to make up. Sanguines are talkative, enthusiastic, curious, eager, and sincere of heart. They make friends easily and don't hold grudges. However, they are sometimes undisciplined, speak before they think, and don't always follow through with their promises.

2. Choleric. Simon, the fiery zealot, was probably a choleric. It's likely that James and John were also of this temperament. Cholerics believe that their way is the only right way; they grab for power and leadership, are self-sufficient and independent. They are strong-willed and unafraid to correct the wrongs of others. They are organizers and goal-oriented. However, they may come across as bossy, quick-tempered, and selfish. They seem to thrive on controversy and arguments.

3. Melancholy. Thomas shows some of the characteristics of the melancholy personality. He was timid and fearful, unsure of himself. Melancholy people are deep and thoughtful and very conscious of details. They are cautious about making friends, but faithful and devoted. They often focus on negatives and see the worst side of things. They are often critical of others and suspicious.

4. Phlegmatic. Philip was probably a phlegmatic. He was a

diplomat in his dealings with others, as evidenced by his encounter with the Greeks. Phlegmatics have a low-key personality. They are easygoing and relaxed, calm, cool, and collected. They are easy to get along with and have a great deal of compassion and concern for others. They are competent and steady, but avoid conflicts. They are hard to get moving, and they resist change.

Playing God

Ron came home after a lengthy trip to find me upset about the actions of the three teenagers in our home. In fact, I started my recital of woes at the train station before the poor man even had his luggage in the car. He listened to me all the way home. By the time he had unpacked, bathed, and eaten breakfast, I had told him all.

"Do you know what your problem is, Dorothy?" he asked.

My tears stopped. I looked at him in disbelief. "*My* problem? *I* don't have a problem! *They* have a problem!"

"Yes, Dorothy, *your* problem!" Ron chuckled. "You're trying to play God to those children. You're trying to make them over into your choleric, workaholic image. There's no way our children are going to turn into the serious, hardworking, always-do-what's-right, get-things-accomplished sort of person you are. They aren't made that way. So why don't you stop trying to change them?"

The more I thought about it, the more I had to agree with him. That's exactly what I had been trying to do—remake the children into my own image.

David was the family clown. He could make us laugh, even when he was naughty. On his first day of school I told him, "You'd better be good, or you'll get a spanking from your teacher!"

He shook his head, rolled his big, brown eyes, and said, "Nobody will spank a nice little boy like me!" And no one did, though he deserved it more than once.

Esther was a quiet, thoughtful girl, but very, very slow. She was always the last one ready for anything, and this tried my patience considerably. However, her room was always clean and tidy. Her drawers were organized, and the bottles on her dresser were arranged according to height.

Stephen was a happy-go-lucky boy whose room was always a disaster area. He had lots of friends and was always ready to go anywhere and try anything. Willing to share anything he had with friends, he was greathearted and loving.

Ron was right. God created each of us as unique individuals. There was no need for me to become so impatient with those who did not share my particular choleric temperament. Things went a lot better when I stopped trying to change my children and, instead, began to appreciate them for the special people they are.[6]

That was more than 20 years ago. My children are now adults, living on their own, raising their own families. I would be less than honest if I told you it is easy even now to keep my mouth shut when they don't do things the way I think they should be done. But I pray a lot and try hard!

Personality contrasts

Another way to look at personalities is to think of contrasting traits.

1. Extrovert—Introvert. Extroverts enjoy people, crowds, adventure, interacting, and becoming involved in the community. Introverts withdraw from people and enjoy the quiet to think about ideas, problems, and emotions.[7] This can cause all sorts of problems with adult children. For instance, an extrovert child may long to get the whole family together for a family vacation near an amusement park. Introverted parents, on the other hand, may decide to take a quiet vacation hiking the Pacific Crest Trail.

2. Thinking—Feeling. Thinking types like to base their decisions on logical, objective reasoning. Feeling types make decisions subjectively, based more on how it will affect relationships.[8] Logical, objective parents find it very difficult to understand the reasoning of a feeling, subjective child.

3. Closed—Open. Some people like to plan ahead and have all the details in place. They like schedules, rules, and definite answers. Others like to leave things open for as long as possible, adapting to whatever comes up.[9] A closed parent who makes long-range plans for a family gathering will find it difficult to handle the adult child who wants to do something different at the last minute.

4. Compliant—Strong-willed. A survey done by Focus on the Family revealed that 85 percent of families have at least one strong-willed child. Compliant children are easy to get along with from birth through adulthood, whether their parents are strong-willed or compliant. However, a strong-willed child seems to cause stress to their parents about 90 percent of the time, regardless of the personality of the parent.[10]

All of the above contrasts in temperament offer opportunities for conflict between us and our adult children. The following quote about Robert Moffat, the famous missionary to Africa, and his son John illustrates the difficulties that can arise when personalities are in contrast: "Temperamentally, father and son were poles apart; the one warm, extroverted, adaptable, with charm and panache, who had made himself—whether he wished it or not—a figure of note in all southern Africa; the other austere, introverted, humorless, earnest, distrustful of public esteem, unwilling under any circumstances to compromise. Each man recognized the other's qualities, neither would openly have wounded the other, but their personal relations were not easy."[11]

It is helpful to remember that we are not responsible for the temperaments with which our children are born. No amount of effort on our part will change them. We are responsible to try to understand them and love them as God has given them to us. We can thank God for them and learn to appreciate them for who they are, not who we would like them to be.

As loving parents we will seek to understand all the ways our children are different so that we can affirm their uniqueness and not get upset when they are not like us. Understanding differences can help us set each child free to be his or her own person, being the unique individual God made him or her to be. Many misunderstandings could be avoided if we would accept the differences of temperament in our children, learn to appreciate each child's uniqueness, and look for ways to meet his or her particular needs.

What can I do now?

1. Take a sheet of paper and divide it into columns, one for each child. Put one child's name at the top of each column.

Under it, write words to describe the personality of that child. You may see characteristics of each of the four temperaments in each child, but one will probably predominate. Is that child like you in temperament, or different from you in temperament?

2. *Learn more about the four basic temperaments.* Two books by Florence Littauer offer more information and tests that will reveal your personality strengths and weaknesses: *Personality Plus* (Fleming H. Revell, 1983) and *Your Personality Tree* (Word, 1986).

Hope from Bible parents

Read the story of Jacob and Esau in Genesis 25:22-27.

"Jacob and Esau, the twin sons of Isaac, presented a striking contrast, both in character and in life. . . . Esau grew up loving self-gratification and centering all his interest in the present. Impatient of restraint, he delighted in the wild freedom of the chase, and early chose the life of a hunter. Yet he was the father's favorite. The quiet, peace-loving shepherd was attracted by the daring and vigor of this elder son, who fearlessly ranged over mountain and desert, returning home with game for his father and with exciting accounts of his adventurous life. Jacob, thoughtful, diligent, and care-taking, ever thinking more of the future than the present, was content to dwell at home, occupied in the care of the flocks and the tillage of the soil. His patient perseverance, thrift, and foresight were valued by the mother. His affections were deep and strong, and his gentle, unremitting attentions added far more to her happiness than did the boisterous and occasional kindnesses of Esau." [12]

1. Divide a sheet of paper into four columns. Label them: Isaac, Rebekah, Jacob, Esau. Under each name make a list for each one of the personality traits you've learned from your reading.

2. All four personality types are represented in this family, each person representing one of them: sanguine, choleric, melancholy, and phlegmatic. Can you now figure out which is which?

---

[1] LaVonne Neff, *One of a Kind* (Portland, Oreg.: Multnomah Press, 1988), pp. 1-19.

[2] Ellen G. White, *The Desire of Ages* (Mountain View, Calif.: Pacific Press Pub. Assn., 1940), pp. 291, 292.

[3] *Ibid.,* p. 295.

[4] *Ibid.,* p. 296.

[5] Florence Littauer, *Personality Plus* (Old Tappan, N.J.: Fleming H. Revell Co., 1983); *Your Personality Tree* (Dallas: Word, 1986).

[6] Dorothy Eaton Watts, *The Best You Can Be* (Hagerstown, Md.: Review and Herald Pub. Assn., 1993), pp. 99, 100.

[7] David Keirsey and Marilyn Bates, *Please Understand Me!* (Del Mar, Calif.: Prometheus Nemesis Book Co., Inc., 1984), pp. 101, 102.

[8] *Ibid.,* p. 105.

[9] *Ibid.,* pp. 105, 106.

[10] James C. Dobson, *Parenting Isn't for Cowards* (Dallas: Word Pub., 1987), pp. 51-60, 226.

[11] Mora Dickson, *Beloved Partner: Mary Moffat of Kuruman* (London: Dobson Books, 1976), p. 193.

[12] Ellen G. White, *Patriarchs and Prophets* (Mountain View, Calif.: Pacific Press Pub. Assn., 1958), p. 177.

Chapter Six

BUILDING BRIDGES

Ella accepted the parcel from the postman and closed the door. She stared at the words printed on the package: "Return to sender." A hard lump formed in her throat and tears came to her eyes. *Not again! Why do they send back our gifts?*

That evening she showed the unopened parcel to her husband, Ben. He sighed heavily. "And the check I sent for Jack's birthday was never cashed."

"But we can't just give up," Ella said. "There's got to be something I can do. I'll make a batch of homemade rolls, the kind Jack always loved. I'll take it over in person. Surely they won't refuse that!"

But they did. The wide gulf between Ella and Ben and their adult children seemed to widen every year. No overture of friendship was accepted. Ella and Ben kept writing, calling, and sending little gifts, even if they were returned.

"We were always hoping and praying our love would someday find a way to breach the empty chasm between us and our son's family."

And love did find a way. It took 10 years, but eventually the alienation ended—bridged by the persistent love of Ella and Ben. Carefully, prayerfully, they rebuilt a loving relationship with their once-estranged family.[1]

Building bridges of love is the task of all parents of prodigals. Picture your bridge as having four pillars. Each one has a letter of the word "love" on it. L-O-V-E. Each letter will stand for one of the things Ben and Ella did to build a bridge of love to their adult children—one of the things you and I can do.

Learn to listen

"The secret of good adult relationships is listening," declares Christian psychologist William Backus.[2] This principle is also found in James 1:19: "Everybody should be quick to listen, slow to speak" (NIV). However, we parents are used to being talkers, not listeners, which sets us up for conflict.

Naomi's experience illustrates what poor listeners we sometimes are. Upset over an argument with her boyfriend, she called her dad.

"Hi, Dad," she began. "Gil and I just had a big argument."

"What about?" Dad asked.

"He said I'm spoiled," Naomi said. "He said I always have to have my own way, and then he walked out."

"What? He has no right to talk to my daughter like that!" Dad growled. "I'll tell him so the next time I see him."

"No, Daddy. It's OK. Please don't say anything."

But Dad wasn't listening. He marched right over to Gil's office and told him off.

"That was no help at all!" Naomi told her friend Carolyn. "I was looking for some sympathy, but I never expected him to actually confront Gil. I think Dad saw Gil's attitude as an insult to him as a parent, so I guess he was defending his own pride more than he was defending me. Anyway, it sure wasn't what I wanted from him."

"What did you want?" Carolyn asked.

After a moment of thought Naomi replied, "I guess I wanted Daddy to reassure me that I wasn't spoiled, that I didn't always have to have my own way. Mostly, I think, I just wanted him to listen and love me. But no, he always has to do something to try to fix things."[3]

Naomi's father was "hearing-impaired," an affliction many parents of adult children have. William Backus suggests there are several things parents do while their adult children are talking that causes them to become "hearing-impaired": thinking defensively, evaluating comments, waiting to talk, planning solutions, looking for faults, and planning their own next speeches.[4]

If we would build bridges of love, we need to learn how to clear our minds of our own agenda in order to focus on what our adult children are saying. We may discover that we have been so busy wanting to tell our children what we think that we haven't been willing to hear how they feel.

Overcoming roadblocks

Imagine for a moment that friendship with your adult child is a two-way street. You want to enjoy your adult child's friendship, and he or she would like to be your friend, too. You both set out on this road called friendship, hoping to meet, but roadblocks bar the way. You try to communicate, but turn around disappointed.

Roadblocks are expressions we use to communicate unacceptance. They are words we use to communicate our desire for someone else to change, to think, feel, or act differently. Roadblocks communicate unacceptance and unfriendliness. They bring communication to a standstill.

There are three basic kinds of roadblocks: judging, sending solutions, and avoiding the other's concerns.[5]

1. Judging. Judging roadblocks include criticizing, name-calling, diagnosing, labeling, blaming, and shaming. The judging roadblocks make a person feel unaccepted and unacceptable.

A graphic example is what Barbara Johnson said to her son Larry when she discovered he was gay. Her judgmental words "I would rather have you be dead than be a homosexual" put an end to communication with Larry for 11 months (see chapter 4).

2. Sending solutions. We parents are particularly good at this. These roadblocks include ordering, commanding, demanding, threatening, preaching, moralizing, interrogating, and advising.

Naomi's father used this roadblock. Naomi resented his jumping in with a solution. It implied that her judgment was unsound. It made her feel unheard, unloved, and unable to manage her own affairs.

3. Avoiding the other's concerns. We avoid the other's concerns by diverting, distracting, arguing, and reassuring, all things we do to try to get our children to stop feeling bad. We change the subject or tell them it's not really as bad as they think. They'll feel better after a good night's sleep, we say. The use of this type of roadblock communicates our desire to withdraw from our children's pain.

Ruth Bell Graham is one who understood that there are times it's better to keep quiet than to erect roadblocks. One of those times came when Franklin was expelled from a Christian college. He confesses to driving home slowly, trying to postpone as long as possible the inevitable meeting with his parents. He dreaded the lecture he knew he deserved.

This was the perfect occasion for erecting roadblocks. He was probably expecting a few judging roadblocks thrown his way, such as "Shame on you, Franklin. You should have known better. After all the money we've spent on your education you've messed up again! Are you ever going to get your act together?"

They could very well have preached, ordered, and threatened, "We've told you time and again, Franklin, that you have to obey the rules! You've got to learn to respect authority, or heaven knows where you'll end up!"

When he got home, he saw his mother standing on the front porch. He says, "I wanted to run and hide in the nearest hole I could find. When I walked up to her, my body felt limp. I barely had the nerve to lift my head and extend my arms for a hug. I didn't need to. Mama wrapped her arms around me and, with a smile, kissed me like always, welcoming me back home."

There was no lecture. The subject of his dismissal was never brought up. No roadblocks were erected. "They knew I had learned a hard lesson, and didn't pile on extra guilt," Franklin says. "I sure didn't need somebody else to tell me how stupid I had been. I knew that all too well."[6]

That day Ruth Graham gave a demonstration in building a bridge of love by overcoming roadblocks.

Vulnerability

Jesus gave up His high position to come and be as we are. He became approachable, but at the same time He opened Himself to attack. He made Himself vulnerable, able to be hurt and rejected. His vulnerability led to His death, but the result was the triumph of the Resurrection.

"As hurting parents, we can find new life, too, in following His example. As we open ourselves to the risk of more hurt, in fact, we most often find renewal in our relationships with problem children."[7]

Love will strip away our layers of pride and make us approachable. We will become vulnerable to our children, willing to show our humanity. We need to let them know that we are not perfect, that we, too, struggle with temptation and problems. We need to confess when we have been wrong. It's all right to let our children know we have made mistakes. Only by being open and honest can we establish a bridge of communication with our adult children.

Don had little communication with his 23-year-old son Cliff. They seemed to be worlds apart. Don felt hurt and unappreciated as a father. Cliff felt unloved as a son. Then Don took a good look at himself and realized that he had made some serious mistakes when Cliff was growing up. He decided to make himself vulnerable, to open up to his son, and tell him how he really felt, feelings he had hidden for 20 years.

He told Cliff, "We had prayed for a child for several years, and then you came. I was thrilled. You were so cute and so cheerful, even when you had the accident that caused your left leg to be crippled. You couldn't do things other kids could do. Sometimes they made fun of you, and that tore me up inside.

"I wanted to protect you, but I couldn't. I decided you'd have to learn how to be tough and take care of yourself. So I left you on your own, forcing you to depend on yourself. Now I see that was wrong. It must have seemed like I was forsaking you."

"You were never there for me, Dad," Cliff said with a touch of anger in his voice. "I hated you for that. I thought you were ashamed of me, that you didn't care what I was going through."

"I can see now that I was protecting myself. I kept busy with my work. I guess I was trying to escape your pain. I even thought of ending all of our lives. I know this was wrong, and I don't blame you for how you feel about me; I guess I don't feel very good about myself. I'm sorry, son. Please forgive me."

It was not an easy scene, but at least Don and Cliff had begun to communicate. Their first few times together were tense, and sometimes Don wasn't sure he could take Cliff's anger. But little by little, they began to enjoy each other's company, to relate as two adults, to understand each other better.[8]

Don began building a bridge of love when he was willing to admit his mistakes and to ask Cliff to forgive him.

Encouragement

"Let us encourage one another" (Heb. 10:25, NIV). Voicing our appreciation is the most effective way to encourage someone. It is simply doing what God did for His Son at the Jordan River, speaking words of sincere appreciation. "This is my beloved Son, in whom I am well pleased" (Matt. 3:17). Words have a tremendous power. A word spoken at the right time can change the whole course of a person's life.

Kate McLaughlin discovered the power of encouraging words. She and her husband, Michael, had been seeking ways to love their son Danny, in spite of a lifestyle that was far from what they wished for him. Although he was openly gay, he had many qualities of which they were proud. They looked for every chance to affirm their continued love for him, to express their appreciation.

One Christmas Danny sent a letter to Michael that said in part, "I've wanted to tell you how it made me feel, the last time you were here, when you told me just before you left that you were proud of me. It felt good, Dad—so good. I felt warm all over and even wanted to cry. . . . I want to thank you. Dad, I'm thankful that you are my father."[9]

Shortly after that, Danny shared the news of his recommitment to God and his choice of a celibate lifestyle. How thankful Kate and Michael were that they had kept the communication lines open, that they had built a bridge of love through affirmation and encouragement.[10]

Tony Campolo also had a mother who was an encourager. He writes, "My mother had a way of minimizing my failures and accentuating my accomplishments. Over and over again, she told me how proud she was of anything I did that had any value. I don't ever remember her saying, 'You could have done better.' Instead, she always made me feel that I had done more than had been expected of me. I would hear her tell her friends,

'That boy of mine is really something. He doesn't have the advantages of most kids in this neighborhood, but look how well he's doing in school. Who would have guessed that my boy would be so successful!'

"Every day as I left the house, the first thing she would say to me was 'Remember! You can go over the top for Jesus!' We joked about that, but the last conversation I had with her before she died ended with those exact words. My mother made me feel special. She made me feel that I could do great things. She convinced me that any limitations in my background could be overcome."[11]

Kate and Michael McLaughlin and Tony Campolo's mother built bridges of love through the use of affirmation and encouragement.

What can I do now?

1. Catherine Marshall once went on a fast from criticism.[12] She wouldn't allow any critical words to escape her lips all day. Try it the next time you are with your adult children. You may find it harder than you imagine, but it is one way to start building a bridge of love.

2. Write a thank-you letter to each of your adult children. In it express your thankfulness that they are your children. Find specific things to appreciate in each child. Let them know how proud you are of them. Do not mention the areas of their lives that cause you concern.

3. The next time you are talking to your child, determine to pay attention to your own performance as a hearer. Tune into your behavior as a listener. How do you respond when he or she is talking? Grade yourself. Make note of responses you made that show you are "hearing-impaired."

Hope from Bible parents

Read the following texts that tell us something about God's attempt to build bridges of love to us, His erring children. Which pillar does each illustrate—Listening, Overcoming Roadblocks, Vulnerability, or Encouragement?

1. Psalm 6:9; Psalm 34:4; Zechariah 10:6; Zechariah 13:9.

2. Luke 15:11-32; Psalm 103:2-5, 10, 11; Revelation 2:2, 3, 9, 13.

3. John 8:11; John 3:17; Romans 8:34-39.
4. Philippians 2:5-8; Isaiah 53; 1 John 4:9, 10.

[1] Marjorie M. Lewis with Gregg Lewis, *The Hurting Parent,* pp. 99-101.

[2] William and Candace Backus, *What Did I Do Wrong? What Can I Do Now?,* p. 125.

[3] Carolyn Johnson, *Forever a Parent* (Grand Rapids: Zondervan Pub. House, 1992), pp. 121, 123.

[4] Backus, pp. 126, 127.

[5] Franklin Graham, *Rebel With a Cause,* pp. 106-108.

[6] Backus, p. 93.

[7] *Ibid.,* pp. 90-92.

[8] *Ibid.*

[9] Kate McLaughlin, *My Son, Beloved Stranger* (Boise, Idaho: Pacific Press Pub. Assn., 1995), p. 138.

[10] *Ibid.,* pp. 140, 141.

[11] Gloria Gaither, ed., *What My Parents Did Right* (Nashville: Star Song Pub. Group, 1991), p. 37.

[12] Catherine Marshall, *A Closer Walk* (New York: Avon Books, 1986), pp. 62, 63.

Chapter Seven

WEAVING CORDS OF LOVE

The heart of 15-year-old Davy Crockett beat faster as he walked the familiar trails near the Nolichucky River in what is now Tennessee. The very air smelled like home. He paused a moment in the dusk before a large weather-beaten log cabin. Several wagons were already parked in the spacious yard. A hand-carved wooden sign above the door read "Crockett's Tavern, Room and Board."

"I can't do it," Davy said, shaking his head. "What if they don't remember me? After all, it's been two years, almost three!"

He remembered his leaving as if it were yesterday. He'd been only 13 and was attending school for the first time. On the fourth day he had beaten up a boy. Fearing a beating from the stern schoolmaster, Davy had hidden in the woods. When his father found out about his truancy, he promised a whipping the next day if Davy didn't go to school. Caught between two whippings, Davy had hired himself out to a man who was about to drive a herd of cattle to Virginia.

Now he was back. What reception would he have? "I'll go in just like any other traveler," Davy decided. "Maybe they won't even recognize me."

And they didn't. After all, they had long ago given him up for dead. It wasn't until they were seated around the supper table that he was recognized.

"Davy!" his sister screamed, running around the table

and giving him a big hug. "Davy, my lost brother! Where've you been?"

"I can't believe it!" his mother cried through her tears. "All this time we thought you were dead! Oh, but I'm glad you've come home."

"The joy of my family at my return was such that it humbled me," Davy wrote later. "It made me sorry that I hadn't submitted to a hundred whippings sooner than cause so much affliction as they had suffered on my account."[1]

The Crocketts knew how to offer grace to a prodigal son. They understood the importance of the cords of love, that mysterious enfolding, drawing power of acceptance freely given.

God's lariat of love

Phillip Keller was born of missionary parents in the bush country of Kenya, but for much of his life he rebelled against the simple faith of his parents, seeking success without God. Through many trials and difficulties God patiently led Phillip back to Himself, and back to Africa to serve as a missionary to the Masai in answer to his mother's prayers. Today Phillip Keller is known to thousands as the author of more than 30 books about practical Christian living.[2]

Concerning God's dealing with him Keller writes, "To put it in rough ranch language, my Master, at last, had flung His lariat of love around me. And now I bore His brand."[3]

"His lariat of love" was Keller's unique way of describing what Hosea calls "the cords of love," the means our heavenly Parent uses to draw His rebellious children to Himself.

"I was the One who took Israel by the hand and taught him to walk. I was the One who watched over him. But the people of Israel don't seem to know that I was the One who did all this for them and healed them.

"I drew them to me with the cords of love and kindness. I picked them up and held them to my cheek. I took the yoke from their backs and bent down to them and fed them" (Hosea 11:3, 4, Clear Word).

"The love of God still yearns over the one who has chosen to separate from Him, and He sets in operation influences to bring him back to the Father's house. . . . A golden chain, the mercy and compassion of divine love, is passed around every imperiled soul."[4]

What a picture of our heavenly Parent in pain! What a picture of love, mercy, kindness, and grace! What an example for parents of prodigals!

What is grace?

Grace is favor that is undeserved; it is the gift of mercy in the place of punishment.

A woman once approached Emperor Napoleon with the request "Please, pardon my son."

"No!" Napoleon replied. "This is your son's second offense. Justice demands his death."

"I don't ask for justice," the mother cried. "I plead for mercy."

"After the crime he's committed, he doesn't deserve mercy," said Napoleon.

"If he deserved it, then it would no longer be mercy," she countered. "Mercy is all I ask."

Moved by the mother's simple plea, the emperor declared, "Well, then I will have mercy. Your son is pardoned."[5]

Grace is a king granting pardon. It is a father running to meet the prodigal. It is the kiss of a mother when a child has been naughty. It is the presenting of a gift to an undeserving, ungrateful child. It is the lavish gift God extends to us as we approach His throne with guilty hearts. It is the amazing message that He is for us, not against us!

Amazing grace

John Newton experienced that grace firsthand in the midst of a storm at sea. Although raised by a godly mother who taught him the Bible, he turned his back on it during his teens. He went to sea and tried to forget his mother's prayers. He discovered he could get a good laugh from his fellows by twisting the words of Scripture into irreverent jokes.

He went from bad to worse and eventually was forced by a press-gang to serve on a naval vessel. He disobeyed orders and ended up serving a slave trader on the coast of Africa, where he became a slave of slaves. He escaped and found passage on a ship to England.

During that trip a terrible storm threatened to sink the ship. Afraid, the captain wanted to throw John overboard, fearing the storm was God's punishment on Newton. John wondered himself if it might be true.

As the waves threatened to capsize the ship, Newton thought of his life of sin and how far he had wandered from his mother's teaching. He felt that his sins were too great to be forgiven, that death was a just punishment he would soon receive. When the storm let up and the ship was still afloat, Newton saw it as a sign of hope. He began to pray for the first time in many years.

The days that followed were still full of danger. They had few provisions, and the ship had lost most of its sails in the storm. There seemed little chance they would meet another vessel. John spent those days praying and reading the Bible, searching for the way back to God. One day he read the story of the prodigal son in Luke 15. Suddenly he saw himself as the runaway in the story and knew the arms of his heavenly Father waited to welcome him home.

That day John Newton accepted God's grace and was born again. He returned to England to become a beloved pastor and writer of hymns. He never tired of telling how God's grace saved him in the middle of a storm at sea. He wrote about his gratitude in these words:

> Amazing grace! how sweet the sound,
> That saved a wretch like me!
> I once was lost, but now am found,
> Was blind, but now I see.[6]

John Newton's life illustrates that the cords of God's love are long enough to reach prodigals, no matter how far they have strayed from home. But that grace is not only for wandering children; it is for wandering parents, too.

Grace for parents

One morning I awoke at 4:00 and couldn't get back to sleep. All my mistakes of the past, my imperfections of character, and the many times I had failed God (particularly as a parent) kept replaying in my mind until I felt completely discouraged. At last I got up and turned to my Bible. I found encouragement in Micah 7:18, 19, where it says that God delights "to show mercy" and hurls "all our iniquities into the depths of the sea" (NIV).

"Thank You, Lord," I prayed with joy. "Thank You for Your love and grace that forgives all the mistakes I've made as a parent. Please, help me to be like You, offering grace to my children. Help me to remember their sins no more, just as You remember mine no more."

Offering grace to our children

Think of what God's grace means to us as parents. Think of how our heavenly Father treats us when we stray from His will. We can do the same for our children. Grace is perhaps the greatest gift of love we can ever bestow upon our adult children.

God's grace is ever gentle, so we will strive to be gentle with the fragile emotions of our wandering children. We will think twice before we speak, holding our tongue from bitter words rather than bruise an already wounded spirit.

Like a soft summer rain, God's grace gives hope to our hurting hearts. So we, through a relationship of mercy and forgiveness, will offer hope to our children.

God's grace accepts us totally, just as we are. So we can accept our prodigals, no matter how much they have disappointed us. We can accept them just as they are now with their strengths and weaknesses, their possibilities and their failures.

In all the disappointments of life, even those of our own making, God's presence comforts us. His grace heals and blesses. So we can be like a soothing balm to our children, offering grace that will comfort, heal, and bless, even when they have brought the trouble upon themselves.

God's grace encourages us with words of blessing, love, and hope, when we deserve cursing, scorn, and death. So we can offer encouragement to our children, even when they do not deserve it.

Grace offers a new beginning

Margaret went to visit her adult son, Greg, and became angry the minute she walked in the door. He was 29 years old and still working at minimum-wage jobs—when he worked, that is. She felt sick at her stomach to realize he was living a hand-to-mouth existence. Half the time Greg didn't know where he'd be sleeping, let alone what he'd eat. His friends let him sleep on their couch or floor when he was out of work. Sometimes he slept in his car and showered at the beach.

"You're just like your father!" she yelled at him. "If you don't get hold of your life, you'll end up as a deadbeat, broke and alone, just like he is!"

"Shut up!" Greg screamed back at her, anger flashing in his dark eyes. "Stop trying to run my life!"

Tears stung Margaret's eyes as she realized that she had done what she had vowed she'd never do—compare him to his father, who had left them when Greg was 8 years old. She turned around and walked out, feeling miserable.

"I've really blown it this time!" she told her friend Karen. "I didn't mean to sound so cruel. But it was as if we were strangers, and I didn't know how to talk to him. He is so stubborn. I don't know what to do."

"You can start over," Karen suggested. "You can acknowledge your mistakes and start over."

"Start over?" Margaret asked. "How? Greg's 29. He'll never be my little boy again."

"I remember hearing a sermon once about our God of a second chance—and a third chance, and a fourth, or more, if need be. He never turns His back on us. I have to believe that He'll give you another chance. He'll make it possible. It can happen for you and Greg," Karen told her friend.

After Margaret was gone, Karen O'Connor thought a lot about the God of the second chance. She writes, "As I drove home that morning, I was overcome with the idea of a second chance and what that could mean to other parents such as Margaret and me—mothers and dads who longed for the opportunity to restore a troubled or broken relationship with their adult children."[7]

And that is exactly what God's grace does. Jesus Christ died on the cross of Calvary to give a second chance to parents and their prodigals. The cords of love are fashioned from the threads of mercy and grace.

What can I do now?

1. Make a list of people in the Bible who "blew it," but to whom God in His love and mercy offered a second chance.

2. Write a love letter to God, appreciating His goodness and mercy in your life. Be specific about the times He has given you a second chance, has shown you love and grace that you did not deserve. Then confess your difficulty in extending the same grace to your children. Ask Him to give your relationship with them a second chance. Ask for His strength to fashion cords of love from the threads of mercy and grace.

3. Each day choose a different text in which the word "grace" appears. Read it in different versions. Write your own paraphrase of the verse, inserting your name. Rewrite it, inserting the names of your children. Here are some verses to try:

Romans 3:24	Galatians 1:6	Ephesians 2:8
1 Peter 3:7	Psalm 84:11	Romans 5:20
1 Corinthians 15:10	2 Corinthians 12:9	2 Peter 3:18

Hope from Bible parents

Read Genesis 22:9-18. Notice that the angel spoke twice in this story, each time giving a special blessing of grace.

1. What were the two blessings?

2. Isaac passed the second blessing on to his son, Jacob (see Gen. 28:3). What memories must Isaac have had as he was giving this blessing? What effect do you think God's sparing his life many years before on Mount Moriah had on his extending the grace and blessing he extended to his son, who had just lied to him and cheated his brother?

3. God repeated the blessing to Jacob at Bethel (see verses 12-15). What does this tell you about God's grace?

[1] Dorothy Eaton Watts, *Stepping-Stones* (Hagerstown, Md.: Review and Herald Pub. Assn., 1987), p. 232.

[2] Phillip W. Keller, *Wonder O' the Wind* (Waco, Tex.: Word, 1982), pp. 13-237.

[3] *Ibid.*, p. 232.

[4] Ellen G. White, *Christ's Object Lessons* (Washington, D.C.: Review and Herald Pub. Assn., 1941), p. 202.

[5] H.M.S. Richards, *The Promises of God* (Washington, D.C.: Review and Herald Pub. Assn., 1956), p. 264.

[6] Samuel Fisk, *Forty Fascinating Conversion Stories* (Grand Rapids: Kregel Pub.,

1993), pp. 105-110; Ruth Bell Graham, *Prodigals and Those Who Love Them* (Colorado Springs: Focus on the Family, 1991), pp. 27-32; Hugh T. Kerr and John M. Mulder, eds., *Conversions* (Grand Rapids: Wm. B. Eerdmans Pub. Co., 1983), pp. 87-91.

[7] Karen O'Connor, *Restoring Relationships With Your Adult Children,* pp. 3-9.

Chapter Eight

MENDING FENCES

For 30 years an old farmer had been fighting with his neighbor over the placement of a fence. Because of the dispute, neither one would mend that fence. On his deathbed the old man decided to make things right. Calling his wife, he said, "Please tell Abner that I'm dying and wish to speak to him."

Before long she was back with neighbor Abner. The old man trembled as he spoke. "Abner, you and me has been feudin' about the fence nigh unto 30 years. I've said some pretty hard things about you, and I want to tell you I'm mighty sorry. I'd like to be friends with you before I die. Will you forgive me?"

"Of course," Abner said, his eyes moist. "I reckon I've said some pretty hard things about you in the last 30 years, as well. Yep, it's time to be friends."

After a solemn handshake the sick man shook a finger at Abner and said, "But mind you, Abner, if I get well you can fergit all that I just said! I'm right about that fence!"[1]

Neighbors sometimes have a hard time mending fences, but if the truth were known, families often have an even harder time. Hurts, injustices, hard feelings, and misunderstandings pile up through the years on both sides of the fence. The older we get, the more we want to mend those fences, but the harder it seems to do. Yet mending fences means restoring relationships, and this is what parents of prodigals want more than anything else.

"Forgiveness is a crucial step in restoring relationships with our adult children," says Karen O'Connor.[2]

There are three ways we can go about using forgiveness to mend our family fences. We can ask for it, we can respond with it, and we can offer it.

Ask forgiveness

For almost 12 years Nell Thompson and her only child, Keith, had been estranged. Various circumstances led him to separate from his family. Even when his father suddenly died, there was no response. Five years slipped by before Nell learned that he had moved East with his family.

"Lord, please help Keith and me to be reconciled," she prayed daily, but nothing happened. She had no idea what to do.

One day, while recovering from an illness, Nell listened to a tape entitled "Keys to the Human Heart," by Gary Smalley. *This message is just for me!* Nell thought. *I can see now where I failed in some ways to meet the needs of my sensitive, musical child. I sure wish I knew what I could do about it.*

"Write Keith a letter," came a soft whisper to her heart. Obedient to that inner voice, Nell picked up a pen and began to write. Tears streamed down her face as the words seemed to flow easily from her pen asking for forgiveness for her mistakes and understanding for her ignorance. She quickly sealed the letter, took it to the post office, and sent it by registered mail.

That same day her housemate, Enola, called friends to ask for prayer support. Together they waited for a reply. Days went by with no answer. Then on Mother's Day a beautiful floral arrangement was delivered to the house. The card accompanying it read "All my love, Keith."

"What a thrill that was!" Nell says.

Soon after that Keith got in touch with Enola and made arrangements for her and his mother to fly back East, where he and his family were living. Since Nell hadn't spoken to Keith herself, she felt rather apprehensive about the trip.

Will Keith meet us at the airport? Will he bring his family? How will they treat me after all these years? she wondered.

When Nell and Enola arrived, there was the whole family—Keith, his wife, and their daughters, who were as tall as Nell herself. Why, they had been babies when she saw them last!

That Sabbath they went to church together. The pipes of the organ vibrated with praise as Keith played. Nell grew misty-eyed as she reflected on how the Lord had truly answered her prayers and performed a miracle. That day was the beginning of a new, warm relationship between Nell and her son.

She writes, "Each day that has passed since has been a joy. God is alive, cares, and reigns—and I have learned firsthand the value of James's admonition to confess our sins to each other and to pray for each other so that we may be healed" (see James 5:16, NIV).[3]

"Without that note of willingness to confess to being wrong, there . . . cannot be any progress," declares E. Stanley Jones. "People who are always right are always wrong—wrong by their very attitude of being always right."[4]

Respond with forgiveness

Betsey Moody had never felt so alone in her life. Not only had her husband died, leaving her with nine children under the age of 16, but her eldest had run away from home. Isaiah was her firstborn, her mainstay, the pride and joy of her life. Now he was gone.

When darkness fell, Betsey trimmed a lamp and set it in the window, as she had done every night since he had gone. *Where is my boy tonight?* she wondered as she busied herself with mending after the others were asleep. *What is he doing? Does he have enough to eat? Has he taken to drink like his father did? When will he return?*

"Lord, please look after Isaiah, wherever he is, and bring him back home," she pleaded on her knees before going to bed to try to sleep. But sleep was long in coming. Tears flowed silently down her cheeks and wet her pillow. Troublesome thoughts crowded her mind. *What did I do wrong? Where did I fail? How could I have stopped him? If only I had not been so busy with the new babies and the struggle to feed and clothe my family . . .*

Night after night Betsey suffered her pain alone while a lamp burned in her window, in case Isaiah came back home. Day after day Betsey sent Dwight to the post office to see if there was a letter from Isaiah. And day after day, the young boy took his time coming home, postponing as long as possible facing his mother's disappointment.

"It's no use," Dwight complained one day. "There won't be a letter. There never is. Why bother?"

"But today might be the day!" his mother spoke cheerfully, ignoring the wrenching pain in her heart. "My firstborn has not forgotten me. Run along now!"

"What makes you so sure?" Dwight questioned.

"God hears a mother's prayers," Betsey answered. "He'll bring my wandering boy home. I know He will."

Dwight didn't argue, but he hurt for her. On stormy nights he could hear her voice crying out to God above the howl of the wind. "Lord Jesus, look after my boy tonight. Keep him safe from harm and danger. Bring him back home!"

On Thanksgiving Day she always put an extra chair at the table for Isaiah, "just in case he should come home."

The months turned into years. Then one day as she sat at the door of her house, Mrs. Moody saw a stranger coming along the road. He had a long flowing beard and looked like no one she knew. He stopped at the door of the house, folded his arms, and began to cry. When she saw those tears she exclaimed, "Oh, it's my lost boy! Come in, son, come in!"

"No, Mother," he spoke through his sobs. "I will not come in until I hear first that you have forgiven me."

She threw her arms around him and cried, "Of course I forgive you! Welcome home!"[5]

Betsey Moody understood that her job as Isaiah's mother was not how to make Isaiah into the perfect son, nor was it even her job to see that he became an exemplary Christian. That was the work of the Holy Spirit. Her part was simply to love and accept and forgive, and that she did with all her heart.

In his book *Love, Acceptance, and Forgiveness* Jerry Cook suggests that if we want someone to be restored, then our part is to offer them three guarantees:

1. That they will be loved, always, under every circumstance, with no exception.

2. That they will be totally accepted, without reservation.

3. That no matter how miserably they fail or how blatantly

they sin, unreserved forgiveness is theirs for the asking.

He goes on to suggest that if we cannot offer a person these three guarantees we will never be able to lead him or her to a restored relationship with ourselves, the church, or with God.[6]

Offer forgiveness

"I can't forgive Pete after the way he's treated us," Oscar told Pastor Smith. "No, sir! The hurt is too deep. When he apologizes and shows evidence of change, then I'll forgive. Right now he doesn't deserve our forgiveness!"

"No, he doesn't," Pastor Smith agreed. "But God asks you to do it anyway." Opening his Bible to Ephesians 4:32, he read, "'Be kind and compassionate to one another, forgiving each other, just as in Christ God forgave you'" (NIV). He continued, "Just as God took the initiative to provide forgiveness for us, so we can take the first step in offering it to others."

"Those are hard words, Preacher," Oscar sighed. "I don't see how I can forgive. You don't understand how deep the hurt is."

"That is another reason you need to forgive, Pete," Pastor Smith replied. "Forgiveness is the only way to heal that deep hurt in your heart. Forgiveness is simply a decision to let go of the hurt, to stop replaying the wrongs that cause the pain."

"I refuse to be a hypocrite." Oscar shook his head. "I can't say I forgive when I don't feel any forgiveness."

"Forgiveness is not a feeling," his pastor corrected. "Forgiveness is a choice we make not to hold a hurt to another person's account. It is erasing the record of their sin in our minds. It is choosing to treat them as though they had never done the wrong."

"But he *did* wrong," Oscar insisted. "I can't condone his behavior."

"Of course not; I don't approve of Pete's actions any more than you do," Pastor Smith agreed. "Forgiveness is simply releasing Pete from your personal judgment, leaving that to God. 'Judgment is mine, I will repay,' says the Lord. Because He is going to take care of it, you don't need to. Forgiveness doesn't mean that you agree with what Pete has done, but that you will no longer hold it to his account. Forgiveness is not a feeling, but a deliberate act of the will. Make the choice, do the action, and the feeling will come in due time."

"I get your point," Oscar admitted, "but Pastor, it still won't be easy."

In fact, it was one of the most difficult things Oscar had ever done. Only through Christ's strength was he able to do it.

Love's toughest work

"Forgiving is love's toughest work and love's biggest risk," states Lewis B. Smedes. "Forgiving seems almost unnatural. Our sense of fairness tells us people should pay for the wrong they do. But forgiving is love's power to break nature's rule."[7] Catherine Marshall is one who would say it is worth the risk.

Catherine faced many challenges when she married Len LeSourd and took on the responsibility of being mother to three stepchildren. From the beginning she found it particularly difficult to get along with Linda. They clashed over clothes, food, bedtime, money, and duties around the house.

Linda, meanwhile, felt that her new mom not only didn't understand her, but had taken away her father as well. She became a very unhappy, rebellious teenager. By the time Linda graduated from college there was a real problem.

Len, Catherine, and Linda spent a whole evening trying to get to the bottom of Linda's problem. Eventually, at her father's urging, Linda got on her knees and confessed her sins of rebelliousness and irresponsibility to the Lord. Tears flowed freely as she accepted God's forgiveness and peace. She got up smiling, then went to both Len and Catherine and asked them to forgive her, too.

However, that night Catherine was unable to sleep. After wrestling with God about her own need of forgiveness, she knew what she had to do. The next morning Catherine went to Linda, her Bible open to the story of the prodigal son.

"Linda, I'm sure you recall the story of the prodigal son," Catherine began. "I have a confession to make. When you received God's forgiveness last night, my reaction was 'All those years of anxiety and turmoil you put your father and me through, and now you're instantly forgiven by God. Isn't that too easy?'

"This morning God gave me the answer," Catherine continued. "God spoke to me and said, 'Catherine, you are in danger of taking the place of the elder brother in the story. Let go of all of those negative thoughts about Linda right now. Furthermore, I want you to confess this to Linda.'"

Linda was at a loss for words.

"So as your brothers would say, I've been properly zapped," Catherine added. "Linda, will you please forgive me?"

How neat that God cares enough about me to speak to my celebrated mom about our problem. Wow! He must really love me! Linda thought. To her mother she said, "Oh, Mom, I'm blown away! Of course, I forgive you. Oh, Mom, I really do love you."[8]

Catherine and Linda embraced; "love's toughest work" had restored their relationship.

The decision to forgive

Nelson Pendergrass and his wife offered David a home when he had none. He was in trouble with the police and headed for a life of crime. The Pendergrasses did their best for David, giving him every chance, offering him all of their love.

Then one day the phone rang. "It's the police," Nelson told his wife. "David stole a car. They want me down at the police station."

"Oh, Nelson! Not again! I thought our love would set him right. How could he do it? Doesn't he know how this hurts us?"

"It's obvious that he doesn't care how we feel," Nelson commented as he turned to go. "Anyway, I'll go see what it's all about."

Nelson found himself gripping the steering wheel hard as he drove down the street. He was angry. *How dare David do this to us?* he fumed. *We are trying so hard to give him a chance, and he goofs up again! He deserves to spend time in jail for what he has done. I feel like telling him to get out of my life!*

Suddenly Nelson thought of his recent accident. He remembered being rushed to the hospital, gasping for breath, wanting to just give up and be done with the pain forever. At that moment a nurse bent over his bed and ordered, "Breathe! You've got to breathe!"

Nelson breathed.

"Breathe, breathe, breathe!" the nurse kept insisting. Each time he forced himself to obey.

I'm alive today because that nurse didn't give up on me, Nelson thought, and his grip on the steering wheel relaxed. *That's what I'm going to do for David; I will not let him destroy himself. I will keep on loving him and forgiving him until he straightens out his life. How ever long that takes.*

Nelson was relaxed as he sat beside David in his cell a few minutes later. "I'm not giving up on you, David, and I won't let you give up on yourself. You're coming home. Mom and I still love you. We forgive you. We are going to get through this together, with God's help."[9]

Today David is a responsible and productive person because Nelson and his wife decided to forgive the past, to focus on the relationship, and to leave the rest to God.

What can I do now?

1. Look up the words "forgive" and "forgiveness" in a concordance. Choose 12 texts to read. Which ones especially speak to you as a hurting parent? Choose one that speaks to your situation and paraphrase it. Put your own name and the name of your child in the text. What message is it giving you about forgiveness?

2. Find a quiet spot where you will not be distracted. Take a blank sheet of paper and write down all the things one of your children has done to hurt you. Be specific.

When you have finished your list, take it to God in prayer, releasing each hurt to Him. Tell Him you want to do for that child what He has done for you, to forgive totally and completely. Ask God to give you the same spirit for your child as is expressed in Psalm 103:10-12.

As a symbol of your release of those hurts to God, set fire to the paper and watch it burn. Ask God to help you never to bring up those sins again, but to give you the grace to love your child as though those things had never happened.

Hope from Bible parents

Read in Genesis 45 about Joseph's forgiving his brothers. Then answer each of the following questions with a yes or no.

1. Is there evidence in this chapter that Joseph refused to play the part of God in judging his brothers?

2. Is there evidence in this chapter that Joseph found it a difficult decision to make?

3. Is there evidence in this chapter that Joseph was willing to let go of past hurts, not holding it to his brothers' accounts?

4. Is there evidence that Joseph was more interested in the relationships of the future than the sins of the past?

5. Is there evidence in this chapter that the relationship with Joseph and his brothers was restored through forgiveness? What about the relationships between Joseph and his father? Jacob and his sons? the brothers with each other?

---

[1] Cecil G. Osborne, *The Art of Getting Along With People* (Grand Rapids: Zondervan Pub. House, 1980), pp. 188, 189; Dorothy Eaton Watts, *Friends for Keeps* (Hagerstown, Md.: Review and Herald Pub. Assn., 1995), p. 155.

[2] Karen O'Connor, *Restoring Relationships With Your Adult Children,* p. 167.

[3] Nell B. Thompson, "Miracles Still Happen!" in Rose Otis, ed., *The Listening Heart,* pp. 157, 158.

[4] E. Stanley Jones, *A Song of Ascents* (Nashville: Abingdon Press, 1968), p. 18.

[5] Gordon Langley Hall, *The Sawdust Trail* (Philadelphia: Macrae Smith Co., 1964), pp. 80-82; Paul Moody, *My Father: An Intimate Portrait of Dwight L. Moody* (Boston: Little, Brown, and Co., 1938).

[6] Jerry Cook with Stanley C. Baldwin, *Love, Acceptance, and Forgiveness* (Ventura, Calif.: Regal Books, 1979), pp. 1-21.

[7] Lewis B. Smedes, *Forgive and Forget: Healing the Hurts We Don't Deserve* (New York: Pocket Books, 1984), p. 12.

[8] Catherine Marshall, *Light in My Darkest Night* (New York: Avon Books, 1989), pp. 138-141.

[9] Gordon and Gail MacDonald, *Till the Heart Be Touched* (Grand Rapids: Fleming H. Revell Co., 1992), pp. 43-45.

Chapter Nine

CEMENTING RELATION-SHIPS

"Oh, if only I could live those years all over again!" Jackie wailed. "I'd do so many things differently! I'd be a better mother the second time around!"

"Me too!" I agreed. "If life had a second edition I would sure correct the proofs!"

But Jackie and I can never redo the past. We can only start with now and do the best we can with the time we have left. There are a number of practical ways by which we can demonstrate our interest and care. These little acts of unconditional love can serve as cement to our relationships with adult children and grandchildren. They are things I can do now!

Our most powerful resource

"Unconditional love is a parent's most powerful resource," states Marjorie M. Lewis. "Unfortunately, many hurting Christian parents never get down to acting out their love, because they are hung up with guilt over the fact they don't always feel the love they know should be there."[1]

It is so easy for resentment, disappointment, anger, discouragement, and other negative feelings to immobilize us from doing acts of love. It is hard to show love when we feel hurt. What we need to remember is that unconditional love is not a warm feeling, but a conscious choice we make. It is a matter of the will. If we make the choice to do acts of love, the feelings will eventually follow.

We need to remind ourselves that unconditional love is given without reservation; it has no prerequisites. It is love freely given with no expectation of gratitude, reward, or even a response. When acts of love are done in such a spirit, they become our greatest resource.

1. The cement of affirmation and appreciation

Our children never grow too old to need words of affirmation and appreciation to build them up, to give them courage to go on with life. They need to hear often that we are proud of them, that we are interested in what they are doing, that we believe in them even when they make mistakes.

They need to hear such things as "You're really special to me." "You are so thoughtful!" "You'll make it; I know you will." "You've got what it takes! Good for you!" "I love you." "I'm proud of you!" "You're doing a good job!"

Try to remember the last conversation you had with your adult child. Try to remember the negative comments you made, as well as the positive words of affirmation and appreciation. How did you do? Plan ahead of time several words of affirmation and appreciation you can give the next time you talk to that child.

2. The cement of written communication

Spoken words of appreciation and affirmation lift the spirit. However, there is something very special about written words of love. They are there to read again and again, as many times as the person needs to be affirmed. Written words are often more powerful than spoken ones.

Daryl left home when he was 21 and got his own apartment so he could live the way he wanted—drinking, smoking, and having late parties. He knew his parents didn't approve of his lifestyle, but he wanted to know they still accepted him. A few days before Christmas Daryl dropped by to see his folks. Sitting in the kitchen, drinking a cup of hot chocolate, and eating some of his mom's Christmas cookies, he said, "How come I didn't get a Christmas card from you guys?"

"I don't send cards to relatives and friends I plan to see in person," his mom explained. "I didn't think you'd expect one."

"Well, I sent you one!" Daryl answered.

"Sorry," Mom said. "I'll do better next time!" And she did. Even when she planned to have Daryl over for a birthday dinner, she still sent him a card and a written note expressing her love. When he had an operation, she sent him a get-well card and a plant, even though she was there to visit him every evening.[2]

Cynthia writes a special note to her children and grandchildren on their birthdays. She tells them several things she appreciates about them. She tells why they are so special to her.

Mark occasionally faxes his son a cartoon with a note to say "I thought you'd like this. I think of you often. Dad."

Marilyn writes little love notes and puts them under her children's pillows when they come home for a visit.

Ted leaves a message for his daughter on her computer.

3. The cement of memories

Ernestine made a scrapbook of certificates, awards, news clippings, and other mementos she had saved to record the happy memories of each of her children. She presented these books to the children on their birthday.

Bernie took several months to go through all the slides and videos he had taken of the children as they grew up. He arranged scenes into a fast-moving video that showed the good times they had experienced as a family. At Christmas each child received a video entitled *This Is Your Life!*

Myrtle prepared a photo album that told the life story of each of her children, along with brief comments of affirmation and history. She gave it as a birthday present. Now she's working on books like this for each of her grandchildren.

When my husband's mother passed away, Ron spent several hours going through her papers. He discovered boxes of such treasures she had kept, remembrances of her children. There were scrapbooks of birthday and Mother's Day cards from her children and grandchildren. There were photographs, news clippings, and grade cards. Ron was surprised to find she had kept a certificate for perfect attendance he had received in first grade. He had no idea she was so proud of that! There was the first letter he had written to her, when he was 8 years old, containing a list of what he wanted for Christmas. And there were all the other letters he had written through the years.

It was evident that these treasures meant a lot to her, for they had been handled much. However, not once had she told him that she had kept those treasures. He had no idea that she had followed his accomplishments so carefully.

These memories, if shared while we are alive, can do much to cement relationships.

4. The cement of special celebrations

"Too often we wait for special events like birthdays or holidays, and then we're rushed," writes Claudia Arp. "We don't have to wait for a big event, but we do have to slow down. Stop right now and set aside some time today. Look at those special people and events that surround you. Think about the next few weeks and see if you can discover some reasons for celebrating."[3]

Family celebrations may not have been a part of your family traditions, but it is never too late to start. Celebrations don't always have to be a party or a dinner at your house. Take the family out, make a bowl of popcorn, bake a favorite recipe, telephone, send flowers, take a balloon, write a note, write a poem, take some photos. The affirmation and recognition, the idea that you care about them is what makes the occasion special.

Why not begin looking for unusual, often passed-by events that you could use as an excuse for a small celebration for some member of your family? Why not celebrate a dog's birthday, the first snowfall, or the return of the robins? Why not have a party when a grandchild's braces come off, a son makes the last payment on a car, or a granddaughter gets her driver's license?

There are scores of good things happening that are worth celebrating! How about an honor your son gets at work, the anniversary of the day you moved to your present home, or the first daffodils to bloom in your garden? How about a dinner for your daughter's promotion, or your son's safe arrival home from a long trip, or a grandchild's baseball victory?

5. The cement of talk and laughter

How long has it been since you got together for a meal, or just to sit around the fire to eat popcorn with your family? How long since you've had a family barbecue or gone on a family picnic? How long since you and your family sat around and talked and laughed together?

These times can become quite strained when a child's lifestyle is causing us pain. It's so easy to get into an argument or to say the wrong thing that often we neglect these times rather than suffer the pain of being together. It will help if you plan ahead on ways to talk, laugh, and have a good time together without getting onto touchy subjects. Here are a few suggestions:

Save your favorite cartoons. Put one on each plate. Pass them around and enjoy a good laugh together. Or have a joke jar. Tell your family to send their funniest jokes and cartoons. Put them all in a jar. When it gets full, invite everyone over for a joke party. After supper, maybe while sitting around the fire eating popcorn, let everyone take a joke out of the jar to share. Keep going until the jar is empty.

Put a question box on the coffee table when the family shows up for a special meal. Children and grandchildren get to put any question in the box that they want Grandma or Grandpa to answer about the old days, when they were young, or whatever.

Have everyone bring three small objects that are reminders of three things (good or bad) that happened to him or her during the past year. Put these items in a special basket. After dinner, take out one item at a time. The person who brought it must tell about it. Each event mentioned will give an opportunity to speak words of affirmation and appreciation to the one sharing.

6. The cement of being there

It was Karen O'Connor's fortieth birthday, and her husband had arranged a surprise party for her at a restaurant. She was delighted when she saw so many friends there amid flowers, music, and a large display of photographs that spanned her life. She hurried from table to table, greeting people. Suddenly she looked up and saw her mom and dad standing in the rear of the room, smiling at her. They had flown from Chicago to Los Angeles to be with her on her birthday.

She writes, "I burst into tears at the sight of these two who, more than anyone else, had taught me that being there is the greatest gift we can give to our children."[4]

The best gift we can possibly give our children is being there for them in times of joy, sadness, jubilation, and desperation—weddings, birthdays, dedications, anniversaries, holidays, baptisms, deaths, moving, recitals, programs, illnesses, operations, games, and graduations. Of course, we can't always be there in person, but certainly in spirit. We can share their lives through phone calls, cards, and letters, as well as by visits.

Sometimes parents will miss a festive occasion to show disapproval of what has been happening in the child's life. Undoubtedly, the adult child already knows of the parent's disapproval. Being absent only drives a further wedge between the hurting parent and the wandering child. Being there shows love and acceptance of the child, not necessarily the behavior. Being there keeps the communication lines open.

7. The cement of kind actions

Suzanne isn't happy about the choice her son Tim has made to live with his girlfriend, but she wants him to know she still loves him anyway. Occasionally she drops by the apartment where they live with a plate of homemade cookies or a pan of fresh cinnamon buns. She's doing everything she can to cement their relationship.

When Alex decided to bring Claudia, his live-in girlfriend, home for Christmas, Bonnie Ahrens wondered how she could stand it. However, she and her husband decided to make her feel welcome and to spend the same amount on gifts for Claudia that they did for their other children. What if Alex and Claudia eventually do get married? they reasoned. We want to be sure we have a warm relationship to build on.

At the end of their Christmas celebration Claudia gave them both a big hug. "I wish our family were as close as yours," she confided.

Bonnie figures her strategy is working![5]

When Greg went into partnership with his buddy Steve to buy a tavern, his parents felt awful. But they let him know he was welcome for Sunday dinner, as usual. When his car wouldn't start, his dad drove across town and helped him fix it. His mom made special goodies to send with Greg to his apartment. They remembered his birthday and had something special for him at Christmas. Eventually Greg came back to God and to the church and enrolled in the ministerial course.

He often testifies, "Their many little demonstrations of love were what kept me open to them and to God and helped bring me back to where I am today."[6]

What can I do now?

1. Write an acrostic of appreciation about each of your children. Use each letter of his or her name to begin a sentence of affirmation and appreciation about that child. Tuck it into the next letter or card you send.

2. For your child's birthday, prepare a booklet with as many pages as years in the child's life. Write a brief sketch of something that happened in that year of life and illustrate with drawings or photographs. It will be the most memorable card your child has ever received.

3. Plan a relationship strategy for each of your children. Make a list of three things you plan to do in the next month to show your unconditional love for each child. Which of the seven types of relationship cement will you use?

Hope from Bible parents

Read the book of Ruth.

1. Make a list of at least five occasions of joy, difficulty, or sadness when Naomi was there for her daughter-in-law Ruth.

2. Read through the book again. Make a list of the many different ways Naomi gave the gift of herself to Ruth. You should find at least a dozen ways.

---

[1] Marjorie M. Lewis with Gregg Lewis, *The Hurting Parent,* pp. 91, 92.

[2] *Ibid.,* p. 69.

[3] Dave and Claudia Arp, "One Minute Family Building," *Today's Christian Woman,* Jan./Feb. 1990.

[4] Karen O'Connor, *Restoring Relationships With Your Adult Children,* p. 182.

[5] Lewis, pp. 73, 74.

[6] *Ibid.,* p. 94.

Chapter Ten

THE GIFT OF PRAYER

The most lasting gift we can offer our children is the gift of our prayers. It is a gift that can be delivered anywhere in the world, because prayer penetrates all barriers of time and space. It expresses our love better than any other gift we could imagine. Its benefits are eternal, and it costs nothing but our time.

The gift that can go anywhere

Amelia Taylor was visiting a friend who lived about 80 miles from her home in Barnsley, Yorkshire. She awoke one morning with her 17-year-old son Hudson on her mind. She'd been worried about Hudson for the past two years. He was a good boy, but didn't know the Lord as she, her husband, and her daughter did. He seemed careless and indifferent to any appeals to his soul. *What if he should be lost?* she thought. *He's my only son, and I love him so. What can I do?*

"Pray for him." The answer came like a whisper to her burdened heart. "Pray for him now!"

Pray? Of course, I can pray! I have been praying every day, but today will be different! I will go to my room and pray for him all day, if need be. I will not get off my knees until I have the assurance my prayers are heard and he has been born into the kingdom of heaven!

For several hours she stayed on her knees, weeping and praying for Hudson. Finally, a sense of peace and assurance settled over her, and she knew her prayers were answered. She got off her knees, praising God for what He had done.

Meanwhile, back in Barnsley, Hudson was all alone at home and bored. While his mother was kneeling beside her bed he was walking around the house looking for something interesting to read to pass the time. Glancing around his father's study, Hudson noticed a pile of tracts and reached for one.

The stories in these tracts are usually pretty interesting, and I can always skip the lesson that comes at the end. Smiling at his clever solution to his boredom problem, Hudson took the tract and headed for the hayloft of his father's barn. He made himself comfortable and began to read. It was a story about a coal miner who was upset because he felt he was too great a sinner to ever come to Christ.

Some friends visited the old coal miner and shared with him the good news that Christ had already borne his sins to Calvary. Suddenly the worried man shouted, "Then it's done! My sins are gone!"

The words Christ spoke on the cross, "It is finished!" rushed to Hudson's mind with explosive force. For several years he had struggled to become a Christian, but it seemed he could not because of his sins. Finally, like the old coal man, he had given up in despair. He now saw there was hope for him, too.

Christ finished it all for me on the cross, Hudson thought. *There is nothing for me to do to make myself better. I must simply trust the work of Christ on my behalf. My sins are already forgiven. All I need to do is repent and accept what He has already done for me!* Right then and there, Hudson fell to his knees and accepted Jesus as his Saviour.

He could hardly wait until his mother returned two weeks later to share his good news. All smiles, he met her at the door. "I've got some glad news for you, Mother!" he said.

"I know, my boy; I have been rejoicing for a fortnight in the glad tidings you have to tell me," she replied. Then she told him about her all-day prayer vigil. She had been on her knees at the very time he was reading the tract in the hayloft!

J. Hudson Taylor became a missionary to China and was the founder of the China Inland Mission, which was based completely on the prayer of faith. They did no soliciting for funds, but relied wholly on prayer for their needs to be met. He had no doubt that prayer is the mightiest force in the universe.[1]

That June day in 1849 Amelia Taylor demonstrated the power of prayer to travel anywhere across time and space to accomplish its purpose. Prayer can go anywhere God can go.

A gift that expresses love

Dick Eastman describes intercessory prayer as "love on its knees." Eastman, who has written several books on the power of prayer, is himself a product of intercessory prayer. In his early teens Dick became involved in crime. Seeing the way his life was headed, his mother began to pray for his conversion.

Dick and his partner Mike had worked out what seemed a very successful plan for snatching purses. They would go to the local swimming pool and walk in the area where the swimmers had put their towels, beach bags, purses, and wallets. Then while the swimmers were in the water, the boys would casually walk by and put their blanket on top of a neglected towel and wallet. After tossing a beach ball back and forth for a few minutes, one of them picked up their blanket, along with the targeted wallet.

This scheme had worked exceptionally well for several Sundays. Now Mike was on the phone. "Come on, Dick, let's go see what we can get today!"

But something came over Dick that day, and he replied, "I'm not going, Mike. I don't want to do it anymore."

"Why, man? Come on! We'll have a blast!" his friend urged.

"I don't know why. I guess I just changed my mind." Dick didn't know himself why he said that, but he now admits it was his mother's prayers catching up with him.

So Mike went alone. Someone sitting on the bank noticed his actions and called the police. Mike was arrested and taken to jail.

"God had begun to answer my mother's prayers," Dick says. Dick Eastman is thankful for many gifts he received from his mother, but none compares with the gift of her prayers.[2]

Prayer is a gift of your time

She had six children for whom she prayed, but Jim, her

youngest, hung the heaviest on her heart. He was a particularly headstrong youth. When he graduated from high school, he decided he had graduated from church as well. He left the church and rejected its teachings, and for seven years lived his life according to his own desires.

Then evangelist Bona Fleming came to town, and a revival came to his family's church. Though they coaxed him to attend, he determined to have no part of it. One evening while the whole family was getting dressed for the meeting, Jim hid on a side porch. At last they were all out of the house, packing into the car for the ride to church.

"Where's Jim?" his brother Willis asked.

"He's not going," someone answered. "He says he isn't ever going to church again. He's through with it!"

Getting out of the car, Willis went back into the house in search of Jim. He called his name as he looked into every room, but Jim remained silent. At last Willis found him sitting on the swing on the side porch. "Aren't you coming with us?" he asked.

"No. I'm through with church," Jim replied, looking down at the floor.

Willis made no reply, but Jim noticed big tears splashing on his brother's polished shoes.

"OK, I'll go just this once," Jim said, getting up.

Because of having to wait for Jim, the family was late, and when they got there the only available seats were in the second row from the front. The song service was going on, and the words and music combined to reach Jim's heart.

OK, God, I'm yours, Jim silently prayed as the song continued. *I accept You as my Lord and Saviour.*

Meanwhile, Fleming had been watching Jim's face. When the song was finished, he walked to the edge of the platform and pointed his finger at Jim. "You! Young man! Stand up!"

Jim stood.

"Turn around and tell these people what God did for you during that last song!"

Jim blinked and swallowed, then opened his mouth and told of the forgiveness he had found when he had said, "Yes, Lord, I'm Yours."

Tears were streaming down Willis's face. His mother was

crying too. The gift of her prayers for seven years had at last done their work on the heart of her son, James C. Dobson, who became the father of James Dobson of Focus on the Family.[3]

About the gift of our prayers, James C. Dobson, Sr., wrote to his son, "I have observed that the greatest delusion is to suppose that our children will be devout Christians simply because their parents have been, or that any of them will enter into the Christian faith in any other way than through their parents' deep travail of prayer and faith. But this prayer demands time."[4]

The gift of our prayers is so precious because of the time it takes to wrap such a gift with our love and tears daily.

A gift of tremendous power

An illustration of the tremendous power of parents' prayers can be seen in the experience of Dr. and Mrs. John Scudder, the first American medical missionaries to India. They had eight sons, and the seven who lived all followed in their parents' footsteps to become missionaries in India. Dr. Ida Scudder, the founder of the Christian medical college in Vellore, was their grandchild, the daughter of their youngest son, John.

"I want all my children to become missionaries," Dr. Scudder told his wife, and together they fasted and prayed for each of them. However, she took a particular burden for them, and made their birthdays a special time of fasting and prayer for their salvation and service. About her, her husband commented, "She literally prayed her children into the kingdom."

The Scudders experienced particular grief with Henry, their oldest. They sent him to the United States for an education when he was 11. They worried about him constantly because he was reckless, impetuous, and headstrong. Every day they faithfully prayed for the Lord to intervene and do what they could not do.

"I feel a great burden for Henry," Mrs. Scudder confided in her husband. "I sense that he is coming to a point of crisis in his life and needs our prayers as never before."

Dr. Scudder agreed, and the two set aside a whole week for fasting and prayer for the salvation of their oldest son.

By this time Henry was finishing his course at New York University. At the close of the term a young man, Dr. Kirk, arrived in the area to hold meetings for the college youth. Henry attended. At the close of one meeting Henry went forward when the call to surrender was made. He grabbed Dr. Kirk's hand and asked, "Do you think there can be mercy for me?"

"Of course," the speaker replied. "There is mercy for the chief of sinners, so why not for you?"

Henry attended each meeting, and one night approached Dr. Kirk a second time. "You were right; there is mercy for me, and I have found it!"

Henry finished his training and returned to India as a missionary, much to the joy and satisfaction of his parents, who had never stopped praying for his conversion.[5]

A gift with eternal consequences

"When we talk with God in eternity, we will quickly learn everything of worth that was accomplished was connected to an intercessor's prayer," writes Dick Eastman.[6] Clayton Peck, Emilio Knechtle, Augustine, John Randolph, Reuben Torrey, and Charles Spurgeon would say amen to that!

"I doubt I would be a Christian today if it had not been for prayer warriors praying for me when I was a reckless, rebellious teenager," declares Clayton S. Peck, who today is a Seventh-day Adventist minister. "I was driving home from a party in the wee hours of the morning when an overwhelming conviction came over me that I was lost. I could not shake it off. It was an unexplainable, oppressive feeling. I was miserable the whole way home. When I walked in the door I found out why. My father was sitting in the living room with his Bible on his lap, praying for me. That night was a turning point in my life. There is power in prayer!"[7]

"My mother's prayers and letters followed me," writes Emilio Knechtle. "From the moment I set foot on American soil, the Lord began to work miracle upon miracle until all the prayers of my mother in Switzerland were answered, one by one."[8]

Reuben Torrey entered Yale to study law. He was soon caught up in worldly living—playing cards, gambling, drinking, dancing, and smoking. He went to church because it was expected of him, but he had no interest in religion.

During his sophomore year things began to go wrong in

Reuben's life. He was not selected by the fraternity of his choice and felt very discouraged and despondent. *Death is the only escape from my misery,* Reuben decided. He reached for his razor, but felt a mighty force holding back his hand. Reuben knew at once it was God giving him another chance at life. For some time he had felt that God was calling him to preach, even though he wasn't even a Christian. He had been resisting that call; now he surrendered.

"God, if You will take away this awful burden, I will preach!" Reuben cried in despair. The burden immediately disappeared. A wonderful, warm sense of the peace of God filled his heart. He went to bed and had the best sleep he'd known in many days.

Reuben A. Torrey became a world-renowned evangelist and the first head of Moody Bible Institute. Reuben knew what had made the difference. He wrote, "My mother, 427 miles away, was praying and praying that I would become a minister of the gospel. And though I had gotten over sermons and arguments and churches and everything else, I could not get over my mother's prayers."[9]

"Our own experience leads us to believe that God will answer prayer," declared Charles Spurgeon, gifted London preacher of the nineteenth century. "My conversion is the result of prayer—long, affectionate, earnest, importunate. Parents prayed for me, God heard their cries, and here I am to preach the gospel."[10]

When Charles was 10 years old, he came under the conviction of his own sinfulness. He lay awake nights, horrified with the thought that God may not have chosen him for salvation. The preaching of his minister father didn't make sense to him, so he began visiting the other churches in town, trying to find salvation. All the while his parents were praying for his conversion.

Then on January 6, 1850, 15-year-old Charles started out in a blizzard for a certain church but had to turn into an alley to get out of the cutting wind and blowing snow. He looked up to see a snow-encrusted sign swaying in the wind. "Artillery Street Primitive Methodist Church," it said. He pushed open the door and went inside, hoping to warm himself for a while. A dozen people sat in the chapel, bundled up against the cold.

Charles took a back seat. When the preacher didn't arrive, one of the members, a shoemaker, stood up to give the sermon. Charles was disgusted. What could such a simple fellow have to say that would be worth listening to? He couldn't even pronounce the words correctly!

The shoemaker took Isaiah 45:22 as his text. "'Look unto me, and be ye saved, all the ends of the earth.' It says, 'Look,'" the man began. "Now, that doesn't take a great deal of effort. It ain't lifting your foot or your finger; it is just look. Well, a man need not go to college to learn to look.

"It says, 'Look unto Me!' That's Jesus talking. He says 'Look unto Me, hangin' on the cross! Look unto Me, dead and buried! Look unto Me, risen from the dead! Look unto Me, sittin' on the right hand of My Father! Look unto Me, sinner, look unto Me!'"

After about 10 minutes, the layman had finished his sermon. He pointed at Charles and said, "Young man, you look very miserable! Look! Look to Jesus Christ! Look! Look! Look!"

Charles did look to Jesus that night, and the burden of his guilt rolled away. Charles accepted Him as his Lord and Saviour. That night his parents' prayers were answered.[11]

What can I do now?

1. *Draw a sketch of a gift parcel, complete with ribbon and bow.* Cut it out. What intangible gifts of love would you like God to give to your child today? Write those requests on the back of the gift. Let that be your prayer for that child today. When you are finished, place it in your Bible where you can be reminded to pray for them often. Make a prayer drawing for each child.

2. *Visit a Christian book and gift store to look for a picture, plaque, or figurine that focuses on prayer.* Wrap it up and present it to one of your children at an occasion when they might be expecting a gift. Attach a note, perhaps to the back of the picture, that says, "Every day you have the gift of my prayers!"

Hope from Bible parents

Read the story of Jairus's intercession in Mark 5:22-42. Of all the people in this story, with whom do you identify at this point in your life? Why?

1. Jairus, interceding for his child?

2. The mother, waiting anxiously, hoping against hope?
3. The mourners and servants, who had given up?
4. The curious crowd?
5. Peter, James, and John, who witnessed a miracle?
6. The nine disciples left outside to await the news?

[1] Clifford G. Howell, *The Advance Guard of Missions* (Mountain View, Calif.: Pacific Press Pub. Assn., 1912), pp. 299-323; David and Naomi Shibley, *The Smoke of a Thousand Villages* (Nashville: Thomas Nelson Pub., 1989), pp. 99-104; Ruth A. Tucker, *From Jerusalem to Irian Jaya* (Grand Rapids: Zondervan, 1983), pp. 173-188; John D. Woodbridge, ed., *Ambassadors for Christ* (Chicago: Moody Press, 1994), pp. 157-162; *More Than Conquerors* (Chicago: Moody Press, 1992), pp. 50-55.

[2] Dick Eastman, *Love on Its Knees* (Old Tappan, N.J.: Fleming H. Revell Co., 1989), pp. 18, 19.

[3] James C. Dobson, *Parenting Isn't for Cowards,* pp. 77-79.

[4] Gloria Gaither, ed., *What My Parents Did Right,* p. 72.

[5] Howell, pp. 177-185.

[6] Dick Eastman, *No Easy Road* (Grand Rapids: Baker Book House, 1971), p. 66.

[7] Clayton S. Peck, "To Rescue Prisoners in a Spiritual War," *Adventist Review,* Oct. 14, 1993, p. 15.

[8] Kay Kuzma, ed., *My Unforgettable Parents* (Mountain View, Calif.: Pacific Press Pub. Assn., 1978), pp. 68-72.

[9] Warren W. Wiersbe, *Victorious Christians You Should Know* (Grand Rapids: Baker Book House, 1989), pp. 74-80.

[10] Charles H. Spurgeon, *Twelve Sermons on Prayer* (Grand Rapids: Baker Book House, 1990), p. 12.

[11] Samuel Fisk, *Forty Fascinating Conversion Stories,* pp. 135-138; Hugh T. Kerr and John M. Mulder, eds., *Conversions,* pp. 129-132; Dorothy Eaton Watts, *This Is the Day* (Hagerstown, Md.: Review and Herald Pub. Assn., 1982), p. 92.

Chapter Eleven

PROMISES FOR PARENTS

Aurelius Augustine was born on November 13, 354, in the little town of Tagaste, not far from Carthage in North Africa. From the moment of his birth, his mother, Monica, began praying that he would become a Christian, instead of following in the footsteps of his pagan father. Monica not only prayed; she carefully taught her young son the principles of her faith.

When Augustine was a teenager, his father sent him to the best schools in Carthage. The boy did well in his studies, but at the same time he succumbed to the temptations of the city and led a wicked life. He took a mistress, who bore him an illegitimate son. He also became involved with the Manichaeans, a religious cult.

Ships from Rome often visited Carthage, which was one of the five capitals of the Roman Empire. Augustine longed to go to Rome and see the world, but his mother begged him to stay in Carthage. One night he told his mother he was going to say goodbye to a friend who was sailing for Rome. Monica went into a nearby chapel, fell on her knees, and prayed all night that God would keep her son in Carthage. However, when morning came she discovered that he had gone.

One day she felt so bad about what Augustine had done that she talked to a Christian teacher about him. When she had finished her story, tears were streaming down her cheeks.

"Go thy way," the teacher said. "God will help thee. It is not possible that the child of such tears should perish."

Monica followed Augustine to Italy, continuing to pray for him. She searched the Scriptures for God's promises to hear and answer prayer. Often she knelt, put her hand on a promise, and asked God to do what He had vowed He would do. For 33 years Monica prayed and claimed God's promises, but she saw little change.

Then God answered her prayers in a remarkable way one day in Milan in A.D. 387. A faint hint of a breeze stirred the leaves of a fig tree outside the small house where Augustine lived with his mother. Its shade cast a cooling shadow on the prostrate form of Augustine as he lay with his face to the ground, clutching at the grass to steady his trembling body. Tears of remorse flowed freely down his suntanned cheeks.

"O God, save me," Augustine cried in anguish. "My sin is greater than I can bear. I want to escape from my evil ways, but I am helpless to do so. I am an evil, wicked man. Unless You save me, I am lost forever, for I cannot break my sinful habits. How long, Lord? How long must I remain in this wretched state? Why can't this be the hour to end my misery?"

At that moment Augustine heard the chanting voice of a child in a nearby house: "Take up and read; take up and read."

Sensing that this was God's answer to his prayer, Augustine picked up the Bible he had been reading when the feeling of his sinfulness had come over him. Grasping the Book with trembling fingers, he let it fall open to Romans 13. His eyes focused on verses 13 and 14: "Not in rioting and drunkenness, not in chambering and wantonness, not in strife and envying. But put ye on the Lord Jesus Christ, and make not provision for the flesh, to fulfil the lusts thereof."

"The moment I read those words, all the gloom of doubt vanished away," Augustine later wrote. "A wonderful peace and security came into my heart, and I knew that I was forgiven. I had no more fear of death, for Jesus Christ was with me."

He went at once into the house to share the news with his mother, whom he knew had never stopped praying for his conversion. With tears of joy Monica watched his baptism in Milan, overjoyed that after 33 years God had fulfilled His promises.[1]

Claiming the promises

"A promise is the handle of faith that we can grasp in prayer," wrote Catherine Marshall.[2]

"It's the word of a Gentleman of the most sacred and strictest honor," declared David Livingstone.[3]

Peter Marshall once stated, "In these pages [of the Bible] are the living words of the living God. These words include a lot of promises, many of them with conditions attached. All we have to do is to meet the conditions, then step up and claim them."[4]

Glenn Coon, author of many books on claiming the promises, says there are 3,573 promises in the Word. He outlines the "ABC" method of claiming the promises.[5]

A = Ask. "Ask and it will be given you; seek and you will find; knock and the door will be opened to you" (Matt. 7:7, NIV).

"It is a part of God's plan to grant us, in answer to the prayer of faith, that which He would not bestow did we not thus ask."[6]

"Every promise in the Word of God furnishes us with subject matter for prayer, presenting the pledged word of Jehovah as our assurance."[7]

B = Believe. "Whatever you ask for in prayer, believe that you have received it, and it will be yours" (Mark 11:24, NIV).

"Talk and act as if your faith was invincible."[8]

"While words express thoughts, it is also true that thoughts follow words. If we would give more expression to our faith . . . we should have more faith."[9]

C = Claim. "Father, I thank you that you have heard me" (John 11:41, NIV).

"So we may ask for these blessings, and believe that we receive them, and thank God that we *have* received them."[10]

"I entreat you to let your trembling faith again grasp the promises of God. Bear your whole weight upon them with unwavering faith; for they will not, they cannot, fail."[11]

"True faith lays hold of and claims the promised blessing before it is realized and felt. We must send up our petitions in faith . . . and . . . take hold of the promised blessing and claim it as ours. . . . Here is faith, naked faith, to believe that we receive the blessing, even before we realize it."[12]

"Whatever gift He promises is in the promise itself. 'The seed is the word of God' (Luke 8:11). As surely as the oak is in the acorn, so surely is the gift of God in His promise. If we receive the promise we have the gift." [13]

The power in God's Word

Gordon and his wife had heard of Monica's determined intercession for her son Augustine and were moved to do the same for their daughter Gail. Gail had turned her back on Christianity, the faith of her childhood, to worship a goddess and to become a practicing witch. A text that encouraged her parents was James 1:21. He writes of "the word planted in you, which can save you" (NIV). They prayed that the Word of God they had planted in her heart would stay with her, and that the Holy Spirit would use it to speak to her.

For years their relationship was very strained. It was painful to visit her apartment and see pictures and objects used in the practice of witchcraft. Her shelves were full of anti-Christian propaganda and satanic rituals. They cried much and prayed much, but they saw no results.

What they didn't know was that several times during those years Gail had distinctly heard a voice speak to her heart. "Gail, I love you!" it said. On several occasions she would catch herself singing a Christian hymn as she walked down the street. She would will herself to stop singing, but in spite of her determination the words would come back to her unexpectedly.

She became friends with a man who was a committed Christian. She attended church with him and found the worship appealing. She bought a Bible and began reading the stories she had known as a child.

One night Gail was alone in her apartment. Bored, she turned on the TV and watched a Billy Graham crusade. His message that night was "Believe or Die." When Pastor Graham made the appeal to come to the front, she knelt there in her apartment and asked God to accept her back. Then she got up from her knees and burned all her books and symbols of witchcraft. She phoned her parents and told them she had come back to God.

Gordon says, "I thought about how we had 'planted' the Word of God in Gail when she was small, and that through the years of her wandering that planted Word remained inside her, exerting its quiet influence as it was quickened by the Holy Spirit. . . . Now we know that God's Word remains inside our children, even when they drift from the Lord. It is capable of bearing fruit again, just as it did in our beloved daughter." [14]

Hanging on to the promises

Ken and Gladys McAllister were heartbroken when Steve turned away from God. However, they began searching the Bible for promises each day, committing their lives and the life of their son to God.

On the morning they heard Steve had been in a near-fatal car crash in Germany, the Lord gave them the promise "Behold, I am with thee, and will keep thee in all places whither thou goest, and will bring thee again into this land" (Gen. 28:15).

Every day after that the McAllisters claimed that verse for Steve. They prayed it, although they knew nothing of his involvement in crime, drugs, and gang warfare. Another verse they claimed regularly was "I know whom I have believed, and am persuaded that he is able to keep that which I have committed unto him against that day" (2 Tim. 1:12). Had not they dedicated Steve to God from the time he was a baby? Surely God would somehow keep that precious life they had committed to Him so long ago. They believed the promise and kept praying.

Sometimes Gladys would wake up in the middle of the night in an agony of despair for her son. At such times she would repeat a promise she had memorized. One that she often repeated to God in prayer was 2 Timothy 1:7, "God hath not given us the spirit of fear; but of power, and of love, and of a sound mind." Another was Ephesians 3:20: He "is able to do exceeding abundantly above all that we ask or think, according to the power that worketh in us."

Years went by, and although the McAllisters saw no results from their prayers, God was working. Once Steve was breaking into an apartment through a back window when someone inside shot at him. He later told how the window blew into bits. He felt the buckshot part his hair, but he wasn't even scratched. At that very moment a Bible verse came to mind: "There shall not one hair of his head fall to the ground" (1 Sam.

14:45). He knew that at that moment his mother must be on her knees praying for him.

Still Steve did not repent. He was speeding with his girlfriend on his motorcycle when a tractor-trailer hit them from behind. They were thrown clear, but the bike was completely crushed. Again he had the feeling his mom must be praying for him, but he said nothing to her, nor did he change his ways.

Once Steve was beaten by a gang of 20 men and left for dead; yet he survived. At least twice Steve was mysteriously kept from completing murders he had planned. He realized later that God's hand had been on him.

When Steve finally turned from a life of crime, it was not to turn to God, but to Zen philosophy. Gladys and Ken continued to pray for their son's deliverance, claiming Bible promises. One night Steve couldn't sleep. He got up around midnight and drove to a quiet lake to meditate, Zen-style, seeking peace and calm. With sudden clarity the words his mother had once spoken came to him: "The only way to the Father is through the Son. He is the Way, the Truth, and the Life."

If Zen Buddhism is true, then Christianity is false, Steve reasoned. *I must decide which way I will go.*

He says, "Suddenly I really believed Jesus Christ was the Son of God. I knew my parents' faith was real because their love was real." He fell on his knees and committed his life to Jesus Christ that night beside that lake.

Steve went to his parents' home for breakfast and told the story of his return to God. Ken and Gladys shed tears of joy at seeing the answer to more than 10 years of prayer and claiming Bible promises. Steve shared with them the many times that God had been speaking to him through the years. Today he is a committed Christian businessman who takes an active part in his local church.[15]

What can I do now?

1. Begin to keep a prayer notebook in which you write out the Bible promises you are claiming for your children. Have one section where you keep a record of indications you have that God is working in their lives.

2. Here are some promises to read in several different

Bible versions. Write them on 3 x 5 index cards. Place them around the house where you can read them often, giving you hope and courage in your prayers for your wayward children. Or put them in a dish beside your bed, and read one each day. Each week choose one to memorize.

Acts 2:39	Psalm 119:90	Numbers 23:19
Jeremiah 24:6, 7	Isaiah 49:25	Malachi 4:5, 6
2 Peter 3:9	1 John 5:16	Hosea 14:4
Philippians 1:6	1 John 2:1	Proverbs 22:6
Isaiah 49:15, 16	Mark 10:27	Hebrews 10:23
Jeremiah 32:17	Isaiah 43:1	2 Timothy 1:12
2 Timothy 1:7	Ephesians 3:20	James 1:21

Hope from Bible parents

Read the story of the Canaanite woman in Matthew 15:22-28.

1. Does this woman follow each of the steps for claiming Bible promises as discussed in this chapter? Does she Ask, Believe, and Claim the promise, receiving the blessing for which she asked? Find evidence of each step in this story.

2. The woman asks for mercy for her daughter, something that God has definitely promised to give. Use your concordance to find Old Testament promises of mercy that she may have known about.

3. The Canaanite woman called Jesus "Lord, Son of David," which shows she recognized Him as the Messiah. Read the blessings of the Messiah as promised in Isaiah 61.

4. Jesus walked 100 miles out of His way to answer this mother's prayer.[16] What hope does this give you?

---

[1] Ray Beeson and Ranelda Mack Hunsicker, *The Hidden Price of Greatness* (Wheaton, Ill.: Tyndale House Pub. Inc., 1991), pp. 3-7; Ruth Bell Graham, *Prodigals and Those Who Love Them,* pp. 3-11; Hugh T. Kerr and John M. Mulder, eds., *Conversions,* pp. 11-14; Dorothy Eaton Watts, *Stepping-Stones,* p. 161; *This Is the Day,* p. 325.

[2] Catherine Marshall, *Adventures in Prayer* (Old Tappan, N.J.: Fleming H. Revell Co., 1975), p. 90.

[3] *Ibid.,* pp. 83, 84 (quoting *Livingstone's Diary,* Jan. 14, 1856).

[4] *Ibid.*

[5] Glenn Coon, *A Study Guide to the Prayer of Reception* (Roan Mountain, Tenn.: Dynamic Living, 1968).

[6] Ellen G. White, *The Great Controversy* (Mountain View, Calif.: Pacific Press Pub. Assn., 1950), p. 525.

[7] —— *Thoughts From the Mount of Blessing* (Mountain View, Calif.: Pacific Press Pub. Assn., 1956), p. 133.

[8] —— *Christ's Object Lessons,* p. 147.

[9] —— *The Ministry of Healing* (Mountain View, Calif.: Pacific Press Pub. Assn., 1942), pp. 252, 253.

[10] —— *Steps to Christ* (Mountain View, Calif.: Pacific Press Pub. Assn., 1956), p. 51.

[11] —— *Testimonies* (Mountain View, Calif.: Pacific Press Pub. Assn., 1948), vol. 2, p. 497.

[12] —— *Early Writings* (Hagerstown, Md.: Review and Herald Pub. Assn., 1945), p. 72.

[13] —— *Education* (Mountain View, Calif.: Pacific Press Pub. Assn., 1952), p. 253.

[14] William and Candace Backus, *What Did I Do Wrong? What Can I Do Now?,* pp. 150-154.

[15] Marjorie M. Lewis with Gregg Lewis, *The Hurting Parent,* pp. 136-143.

[16] See Ellen G. White, *The Desire of Ages,* p. 400.

Chapter Twelve

REASONS FOR HOPE

"Where there's life, there's hope," one mother told me not long ago. "I just keep praying and loving; that's all I can do. The rest is up to God."

We parents of prodigals hope because we must. Our "hope is like the sun, which, as we journey toward it, casts the shadow of our burden behind us."[1] Hope causes us to look beyond the discouragement of the present to the possibility of a brighter tomorrow. And there are at least seven reasons we have for hope.

1. God's ability to work depends on His resources, not ours.

His resources are unlimited. With God, all things are possible. He has "infinite resources at His command."[2] Even the most complicated personal problems are not beyond God's power. "There is no chapter in our experience [or our children's experience] too dark for Him to read; there is no perplexity too difficult for Him to unravel."[3]

A case in point is Darlene. During her college years she gave up her Christian faith and opted for a lesbian lifestyle. Her parents had no success in trying to reason with her. However, when one of her best friends joined a cult, Darlene began to read her Bible, looking for ammunition with which to argue with him. In the process she convinced herself that Christ's claims are true.

Darlene has recommitted her life to God and is back in church. She has been reconciled to her parents. All her problems have not disappeared, but she is striving to become the person God wants her to be. For Darlene and her parents the assurance is that "God would send every angel in heaven to the aid of such a one, rather than allow him [her] to be overcome."[4]

2. God can use anything to accomplish His purpose for our children.

We are told that "in all things God works for the good of those who love him" (Rom. 8:28, NIV). God is able to work through any and all circumstances for the good of our children and for their eternal salvation.

In the case of Adoniram Judson, God worked through the very same friend who had led him to turn his back on God. Eames, a witty college friend, had debated in favor of atheism, Voltaire, and French infidelity. Convinced by his arguments, Adoniram declared that he was an atheist. His godly parents were upset, but vowed to continue praying for him.

Several months later Adoniram was booked into a small country hotel. The owner called Adoniram aside. "I thought I should tell you that there's a young man dying in the room next to yours," he whispered. "The doctor says he will be gone before morning. I do hope this will not disturb you. The walls are quite thick, and I don't anticipate any trouble."

"Oh, that's dreadful!" Adoniram shuddered as he thought of someone dying so close to him. "But I expect I'll sleep well after my long trip."

The next morning he asked the owner, "Well, did the man die, as the doctor predicted?"

"Yes," the landlord said.

"What was his name?"

"Eames," the man replied.

Adoniram turned pale and hurried from the room lest he faint. The dead man had been his best friend in college, the very one who had influenced Adoniram to give up his faith in God.

"He's gone into eternity," Judson moaned. "He died without God and without hope. That could have been me!" In that moment Adoniram knew he believed, and that someday he, too, must face his Maker. He gave his heart to God and returned to school to study for the ministry. He became a pioneer missionary to Burma (Myanmar).[5]

Adoniram's experience illustrates the truth that God can use any situation, as dark as it may seem, to reach our children.

3. Whether we see Him or not, God is working.

As far as Mrs. Thatcher could see, things were about as bad with her son Phil as they could get. She sat in the visitor's room at San Quentin and waited for her boy. He'd been in and out of jail since he was 11. He looked sullen as he shuffled into the room escorted by a guard, and took his place opposite her. As they talked, a guard kept a machine gun pointed steadily at them.

"Son, when are you going to quit this life of crime and begin to really live?" she asked, sorrow in her eyes.

Phil shrugged and looked down.

"God loves you, Phil. He can make everything better if you'll only give Him a chance," she went on.

Phil sighed and nodded, but made no promises.

After four years he was released, only to get caught again within 60 days. He was 31 years old now and during the past 20 years had spent as much time in jail as out. This time he had no hope of parole for 20 years. That night in his cell Phil suddenly felt homesick. He remembered the prayer his mother had taught him when he was a toddler: "Now I lay me down to sleep . . ." He closed his eyes and whispered the prayer. Somehow it made him feel closer to his mom.

One night he returned to his cell to discover a Bible on his bunk. He tossed it onto a shelf above the door and cursed whoever had put it on his bed. Still, the sight of the Bible brought back a flood of memories. He thought of the Bible verses his mother had taught him. Angrily, he tried to curse them away, but he could not.

Several nights later he waited until his cell mate was asleep, then crawled out of bed and reached for the Bible. Standing close to the door where a sliver of light fell, he began to read. Night after night he read through the Bible until he came to the place that told of Christ dying on the cross. Phil thought of his mother and knew she was praying for him, maybe even at that moment. He lay on his bunk and cried and cursed, but the picture of Christ on the cross wouldn't leave him. At last he prayed, "God—if there is a God—please, show me."

Immediately he thought he heard someone say, "The blood of Jesus Christ, His Son, cleanseth us from all sin."

"O God, You did this for me! What am I to do?"

Softly the Holy Spirit spoke to his heart. "Phil, just ask Me to forgive you."

Phil knelt on the cold cement floor and prayed, "God, be merciful to me a sinner, and save me. For Jesus' sake, amen."

And all this time his faithful mother was praying, having no idea how God was working in her son's heart.

Later Phil received a pardon from the governor of California and began a ministry among delinquent youth and prison inmates.[6]

4. Our children cannot stray beyond the reach of God.

It isn't easy to run away from God. Glenn Aufderhar knows by experience. He quit school during his eighth-grade year, left home, and tried to leave God. But the Holy Spirit followed him to the sawmill, where he'd gotten a job. One Friday night the Holy Spirit shadowed Glenn as he and his friends headed for a theater. He saw Glenn puffing on his Red Dog cigar, trying to act cool.

The Holy Spirit came near Glenn as he stopped in front of the theater to read the posters, just at sunset. As he glanced up at the setting sun, God's Spirit brought back to his memory a Friday evening worship when he was 5 years old. The story that night was about the trial of Jesus. How little Glenn wished he could change the outcome of the story! He didn't want Jesus to suffer. He didn't want Jesus to be crucified on that cross. He ran to the cookstove and grabbed a few sticks of kindling.

"If I'd been there, things would have been different!" Glenn cried, holding the sticks as if they were spears. "I would have protected You, Jesus!"

Standing in front of the theater, remembering, Glenn felt overcome with emotion. He threw his cigar on the ground, and without a word he left his friends. He didn't even turn around to see how they reacted to his sudden departure.

That night Glenn heard God's Spirit speaking to his heart as he looked at the sunset. He knew God was calling him. In his heart Glenn responded, *Yes, Lord, I am coming back to You. I'll do whatever You want me to do with my life.*

God led Glenn back into the church and back to school. He became a minister, evangelist, church administrator, and eventually, the president of the Adventist Media Center.[7]

Psalm 139 assures us that our children can never get away from God. "Where can I go from your Spirit? Where can I flee from your presence? If I go up to the heavens, you are there; if I make my bed in the depths, you are there" (Ps. 139:7, 8, NIV). What wonderful words of hope!

5. God doesn't view time as we view it.

Ken and Gladys McAllister (see chapter 11) waited 10 years for Steve to come to his senses. Ella and Ben, whose son kept returning their gifts (see chapter 6), also waited 10 years. Barbara Johnson (see chapter 4) waited 11 years before Larry came back to the Lord and to a relationship with them. Nell Thompson (see chapter 8) was estranged from her son Keith for 12 years.

Monica waited 33 years to see an answer to her prayers for Augustine (see chapter 11), hard years filled with heartache and tears, when she could do nothing but pray, love, and wait.

Waiting is hard for us, but God is patient. From His perspective of eternity, He is willing to wait the years necessary to accomplish His task. He knows when the time is right, and will patiently work with our children for as long as it takes.

6. We serve a God who gives second chances.

It appears there are several peak times in the "returning curve," as Tom Bisset calls it in his book *Why Christian Kids Leave the Faith.* One of these occurs in the mid-20s, when the young adult is establishing his or her home and career. In a survey of children who leave the church, James Dobson found that 85 percent return to their parents' religious faith and values by the time they are 24 years old.

The next peak is around the age of 40, when the prodigal's own children are entering their teens. This is a typical period of midlife crisis or reevaluation of life. This is a time when many look again with renewed interest in spiritual matters.

Another peak comes along when many realize their immortality for the first time. When illness or some other tragedy stops them short, and they begin to take stock of their future, which they now realize is not forever.

Another prime time for returning comes at the death of one of the parents. Once again there is a tendency to reevaluate one's life and to make some changes.[8]

Trish is an example of God's mercy in giving chance after chance to our wandering children. She ran away from home before she finished high school, got involved in the drug culture, had an abortion, and watched her boyfriend commit suicide.

At her job in a bank Trish had two chances when two of her associates, who were Christians, tried to witness to her. She ignored their appeal. A third chance came when a cousin accepted Christ and tried to share her love for the Lord. Trish wasn't listening.

She got a fourth chance while watching the *Oprah Winfrey Show*. The subject was on demon possession. Trish listened to the story of a woman who tried to kill her baby while possessed by a demon, but who was finally freed through the power of Jesus Christ. Suddenly Trish realized that Satan was real and alive, and that he had been busy trying to destroy her life through drinking, drugs, and illicit sex. She knelt on her bedroom floor beside the TV and cried to God to come into her life and save her.

"My father kept praying for me," Trish says. "And God kept speaking to me, giving me chances to find Him until I finally listened."[9]

7. God will keep on working, even after we are gone.

Dr. W. P. MacKay was working in a hospital in Scotland when a bricklayer's assistant was brought into the emergency room. He had fallen from a ladder, and Dr. MacKay could see at once that his case was hopeless. He proceeded to do what he could to ease the man's intense pain.

"How long have I got, Doc?" the man asked.

"I can't say for sure," the doctor hedged, "but not long."

"Aye, God knows best," the man said, trying to smile.

"Have you any relatives whom we could notify?" the doctor asked.

The injured man shook his head. "I do wish, though, that you'd let my landlady know I'm here," he said. "I owe her a little money, and I'd like to settle that."

"All right," the doctor nodded.

"And tell her to bring the Book," he whispered.

"What book is that?" Dr. MacKay asked.

"Oh, she'll know," the man said, and drifted off to sleep.

Dr. MacKay visited his patient daily and noticed that in spite of his pain the man seemed calm and almost cheerful. After a week of struggle, he died. The doctor was there as the attendants were removing the body and cleaning out the room.

"What shall we do with this?" a nurse asked, holding up a tattered book.

"What book is that?" Dr. MacKay asked.

"The poor chap's Bible," she replied. "His landlady brought it to him, and he read it as long as he was able. After that he kept it close to him, under the bedcover."

Dr. MacKay reached for the Bible and turned the ragged cover to the flyleaf. He gasped. There was *his* name, W. P. MacKay, written in the hand of his own mother! She had given it to him when he left home, urging him to read it daily. He had cast it aside, then when he was in medical school and in a pinch for funds, he had sold it for a small amount. Sudden emotion welled up in the doctor's heart as he thought of his mother, now dead, who had prayed for him for so many years.

"This book is about gone and not worth much," the doctor told the nurse. "Don't worry; I'll take care of it and the other things as well."

Dr. MacKay took the Bible to his room and leafed through the sacred pages. Some were loose; others were torn. It showed evidence that it had been read often. Many texts were underlined. As he read these he could almost hear his mother's voice reciting those verses, just as she had in his childhood.

Tears streamed down the doctor's face as he thought of his mother's love, and for the first time in many years he thought of the love of his Father in heaven. Writing of that experience, he said, "The voice of my conscience could no longer be silenced. I found no rest until I arose and came to Him whose hand of love I had so often repulsed, but who ever thought of me in pity and compassion. By God's mercy and grace I was enabled to believe that 'Christ Jesus came into the world to save sinners,' of whom I seem to be the chief." [10]

What can I do now?

1. Catherine Marshall talks about the "eggs" prayer in her book Adventures in Prayer. She suggests that we turn our hopes and dreams into prayers and write them on slips of paper cut in egg shapes, symbolizing our willingness to let God "hatch them out" in His own time. She did this for her children and tucked them away, forgetting about them until one day she came across the slips of paper in an old Bible. She was amazed that a loving Father had fulfilled every single request!

David seemed to know about the principle of eggs prayers when he wrote, "Wait on the Lord: be of good courage, and he shall strengthen thine heart: wait, I say, on the Lord" (Ps. 27:14). We can bring our requests to God, trusting Him to work things out in His own time. Here is how to use eggs prayers:

a. Write each intercessory prayer on a piece of paper, cut it into an egg shape to symbolize your willingness to let God "hatch" it in His own time.

b. Hide the prayers in a safe place, showing your trust in God to do whatever He thinks is best with those prayers when the time is right.

c. After several weeks, months, or years take them out. You will be amazed at how God has worked.

d. Consider those prayers that have not yet "hatched." Are they still a deep desire of your heart? Then put them back and wait.

e. Make a nest of eggs for each family member. Write the name of a loved one on each egg. Under the name write one desire that you have for that person. Turn the egg over and write a promise that you are claiming for that person. Put your prayer eggs away and let them hatch. Praise Him for every indication the eggs are cracking! [11]

Hope from Bible parents

Read the story of the importunate widow in Luke 18:1-8.

1. Which of the seven reasons for hope do you find illustrated in this parable? Find statements that back up your list.

2. We are told that often the wavering faith of the disciples was strengthened by the memory of this parable.[12] How might it strengthen your faith while you are interceding for your children?

3. Read the following texts. How do they back up the message of this parable?

Ephesians 3:20   Isaiah 45:3
1 Corinthians 2:9   Hebrews 4:16
Ephesians 2:6, 7   Romans 8:32
1 Timothy 6:17

---

[1] S. Smiles, in Tryon Edwards, comp., *The New Dictionary of Thoughts* (New York: Standard Book Co., 1948), p. 263.

[2] Ellen G. White, *The Ministry of Healing,* p. 49.

[3] —— *Steps to Christ,* p. 100.

[4] —— *Testimonies,* vol. 7, p. 17.

[5] Faith Coxe Bailey, *Adoniram Judson: Missionary to Burma* (Chicago: Moody Press, 1955), pp. 7-17; Samuel Fisk, *More Fascinating Conversion Stories* (Grand Rapids: Kregel Pub., 1994), pp. 63-68; Dorothy Eaton Watts, *Stepping-Stones,* p. 349.

[6] Fisk, pp. 151-154.

[7] Gloria Bentzinger, "A Renegade Reclaimed," Adventist Media Center, *Update,* Spring/Summer 1993, pp. 5, 6; Dorothy Eaton Watts, *Friends for Keeps,* p. 61.

[8] Tom Bisset, *Why Christian Kids Leave the Faith,* pp. 146-151.

[9] *Ibid.,* pp. 210-212.

[10] Wilber Konkel, *Living Hymn Stories* (Minneapolis: Bethany House, 1982), pp. 16-19.

[11] Dorothy Eaton Watts, *Prayer Country* (Boise, Idaho: Pacific Press Pub. Assn., 1993), pp. 28, 29.

[12] Ellen G. White, *The Desire of Ages,* p. 495.

Also by Dorothy Eaton Watts

Never Thirst Again gives you hundreds of ideas for adding more joy and meaning to your Bible study and bringing you a greater sense of God's presence. Hear God's voice speaking to you through Scripture. Get to the heart of the Bible author's meaning. Delve into Bible promises that meet your unique needs.

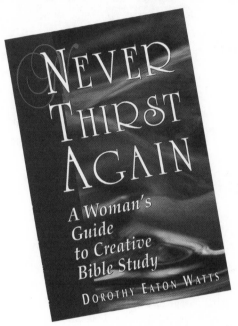

Paper, 127 pages.
US$8.99, Cdn$12.99.

An Exciting Way
to Organize
Your Prayer Life

Make your prayer life more meaningful with this creative new approach by Nancy Van Pelt. In *My Prayer Notebook* she helps you to focus on a specific type of prayer request each day of the week. For example, she suggests that you pray for your spouse on Monday, your child on Tuesday, etc.

My Prayer Notebook will give you a way to organize your prayer requests and answers, and will deepen your faith in God as you see His leading in your life.

My Prayer Notebook includes
- ❦ A beautiful three-ring binder to enhance your devotional time.
- ❦ 128 ruled pages for recording your prayer requests, sermon notes, Bible study notes, etc.
- ❦ Dividers for the days of the week.
- ❦ Dividers for Bible study notes, answered prayers, sermon notes, favorite Scripture, plus two blanks.
- ❦ Instructions on how to personalize and use your prayer notebook.
- ❦ Tips on making personal devotion time more enjoyable.
- ❦ Creative ideas for Bible study.
- ❦ Refill sheets available.

US$17.99, Cdn$25.99.

Add more meaning
to your prayer life

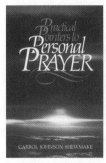

Practical Pointers to Personal Prayer
Carrol Johnson Shewmake guides you step-by-step toward satisfying communion with your heavenly Father. She tells how she lost the boredom and guilt that choked her lifeline to God and instead found intimate two-way conversation. Paper, 128 pages.

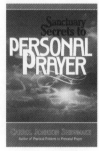

Sanctuary Secrets to Personal Prayer
This book introduces you to a unique prayer experience that takes you through the steps performed by the priests in the Old Testament sanctuary service. Paper, 92 pages.

Sensing His Presence, Hearing His Voice
Discover how you can cultivate hearing the voice of God and have a continual sense of His presence. Paper, 140 pages.

When We Pray for Others
Learn how to begin an intercessory prayer ministry that will bring greater joy and closeness to God. Ideal for individual or small group study. Paper, 128 pages.

These books by Carrol Johnson Shewmake are US$7.99, Cdn$11.49 each.
